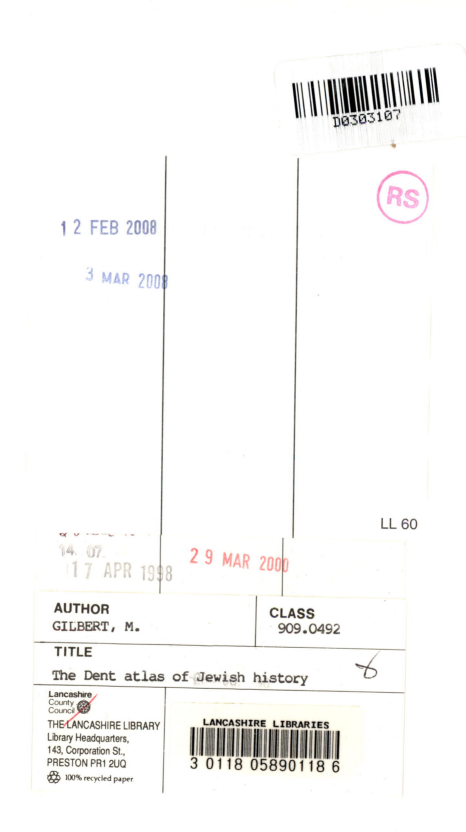

THE DENT ATLAS OF JEWISH HISTORY

OTHER BOOKS BY MARTIN GILBERT

The Churchill biography
Volume III, 'The Challenge of War', 1914–1916
Volume III, Documents, Parts I and II
Volume IV, 'The Stricken World', 1917–1922
Volume IV, Documents, Parts I, II and III
Volume V, 'The Prophet of Truth', 1922–1939
The Exchequer Years, Documents, 1922–1929
The Wilderness Years, Documents, 1929–1935
The Coming of War, Documents, 1936–1939
Volume VI, 'Finest Hour', 1939–1941
At the Admiralty, Documents, 1939–1940
Volume VII, 'Road to Victory', 1941–1945
Volume VIII, 'Never Despair', 1945–1965

Historical works
The Appeasers (with Richard Gott)
The European Powers, 1900–1945
The Roots of Appeasement
Britain and Germany Between the Wars (documents)
Plough My Own Furrow: the Life of Lord Allen of Hurtwood (documents)
Servant of India: Diaries of the Viceroy's Private Secretary (documents)
Sir Horace Rumbold: Portrait of a Diplomat
Churchill: a Photographic Portrait
Churchill's Political Philosophy
Auschwitz and the Allies
Exile and Return: the Struggle for Jewish Statehood
The Jews of Hope: the Plight of Soviet Jewry Today
Shcharansky: Hero of our Time
Jerusalem: Rebirth of a City, 1838–1898
Final Journey: the Fate of the Jews in Nazi Europe
The Holocaust: the Jewish Tragedy
The Second World War
Churchill, A Life

Atlases
Dent Atlas of American History
Dent Atlas of the Arab–Israeli Conflict
Dent Atlas of British History
Dent Atlas of the First World War
Dent Atlas of the Holocaust
Dent Atlas of Recent History (*in preparation*)
Dent Atlas of Russian History
The Jews of Arab Lands: Their History in Maps
The Jews of Russia: Their History in Maps
Jerusalem: Illustrated History Atlas
Children's Illustrated Bible Atlas

THE DENT ATLAS OF JEWISH HISTORY

Fifth edition

Martin Gilbert

Fellow of Merton College, Oxford

JM Dent

*Dedicated to the memory of Terry Bicknell,
cartographer and friend.*

© 1969, 1976, 1985, 1992, 1993 Martin Gilbert

First published 1969
Second edition 1976
Reprinted 1978
Reprinted 1981
Third edition 1985
Reprinted 1986
Reprinted 1988
Fourth edition 1992
Fifth edition 1993

Printed and bound in Great Britain by
Butler & Tanner Ltd, Frome and London

J M Dent Ltd
The Orion Publishing Group
Orion House
5 Upper St Martin's Lane
London WC2H 9EA

British Library Cataloguing-in-Publication Data

A catalogue record for this book is available from the British Library.

ISBN 0 460 861816 (hardcover)
ISBN 0 460 861824 (paperback)

Preface

This atlas traces the worldwide Jewish migrations from ancient Mesopotamia to modern Israel. It seeks to follow the diverse – and sometimes obscure – path of a far-ranging people, and to map their strange experiences in good times and bad.

My original concern was to avoid undue emphasis upon the many horrific aspects of Jewish history. I wished to portray with equal force the construction, achievements and normalities of Jewish life through almost four thousand years. In part I believe that I have succeeded; for there are many maps of traders, philosophers, financiers, settlers and sages. But as my research into Jewish history progressed, I was surprised, depressed, and to some extent overwhelmed by the perpetual and irrational violence which pursued the Jews in every century and to almost every corner of the globe. If, therefore, persecution, expulsion, torture, humiliation, and mass murder haunt these pages, it is because they also haunt the Jewish story.

But not all these terrors are unmitigated; and I have felt a great relief in being able also to map the other side of the coin – the Jewish revolts against Roman, Chinese and Persian oppression – the often repeated pattern of mutual self-help and communal charity, the self-defence leagues organized against the Russian and Ukrainian pogroms, the brave if hopeless risings in ghetto and concentration camp during the Nazi era, and the stubborn resistance to Arab pressures by modern Israel.

If this atlas can help to answer even a small portion of the questions which Jews so often ask about themselves, or can tell Christians something more about the varied experiences of their neighbours, it will have served a purpose. In particular, I hope that the maps succeed in portraying the complex comings and goings of many different sorts of Jews, and the extraordinary diversity of the Jewish saga.

In this atlas I have tried to look at the role of the Jews in their different national settings, and show their reaction to persecution, whether by dispersal, acceptance or defence. Both in resisting the continual pressure of hostile societies and in braving the dangers of flight and exile, the Jewish people have shown high courage and a keen capacity to rise again; "trampled into the dust" as Cardinal Manning described it, "and yet never combining with the dust into which it is trampled."

For those who wish to follow up some of the themes covered by the maps, I have provided a short bibliography. In it I have included a few general books, together with a number of specialist works in which I found information for remote or neglected topics.

Many of my maps are intended to make certain obscure episodes in Jewish history better known, if only in outline. There are many equally fascinating problems on which no detailed research has yet been done; and the history of the Jews which most people know is primarily the history of these episodes on which books and monographs have been written. There are still many areas of darkness. But, as I hope this atlas shows, those aspects of Jewish history which can be mapped are full of unusual details and dramatic moments, ranging over every continent and every civilization, and adding a unique dimension to the story of mankind.

Twenty-four years have now passed since the first edition of this atlas. The final maps of this fifth edition show the main developments in Jewish history since then. These include the emigration of more than half a million Jews from the Soviet Union to Israel between 1970 and 1990 (map 122). This map also shows Operation Solomon, which, with Operation Moses (map 119), brought more than 25,000 Ethiopian Jews to Israel.

I have brought up to date the map showing the number of non-Jews who were honoured for saving Jewish lives in the Second World War (map 104), and the map showing the number of Jews worldwide: this shows the Jewish population of Israel reaching four million in 1991 (map 123). I have mapped, for the year 1992, the continuing immigration of Jews to Israel from all over the Jewish world (map 125), and from the former Soviet Union (map 126). Three new maps (maps 124, 130 and 131) show the spread of anti-semitic incidents in 1991 and 1992. Three more (maps 127, 128 and 129) show the revival of Jewish education and culture inside the former Soviet Union. I have also added a map (132) showing the Jews in the new and warring republics of the former Yugoslavia.

Several of the earlier maps have been redrawn with extra material, including a map showing Blood Libel accusations in the Middle Ages and beyond, two maps showing the scale of Jewish resistance during the Holocaust, and a map giving the numbers of non-Jews who were honoured for saving Jewish lives between 1939 and 1945.

I am grateful in this new edition to the cartographic skills of Tim Aspden and Guy Baker, and I should once more welcome any notice of errors, as well as suggestions for further maps.

26 March 1993

MARTIN GILBERT
Merton College, Oxford

You may say you have been oppressed
and persecuted – that has been your
power! You have been hammered into
very fine steel, and that is why you
have never been broken.

LLOYD GEORGE IN 1925

Maps

EARLY JEWISH MIGRATIONS ABOUT 2000 BC

"I will make of thee a great nation, and I will bless thee, and make thy name great. . . .
And I will bless them that bless thee, and curse him that curseth thee"

The Lord to Abraham GENESIS 12, 2-3

HITTITE EMPIRE

Tarsus

Alalakh
Ugarith
SYRIA
Carchemish
Haran

Death of Abraham's father

Hamath

Byblos
Tyre
CANAAN
Hebron
Death of Abraham

GOSHEN
On
Memphis
E G Y P T
Nile

The Great Sea
(Mediterranean)

0   Miles   200   (Red Sea)

ASSYRIA
Niniveh
Asshur
MESOPOTAMIA
Mari
Euphrates
Tigris
Babylon
BABYLONIA
OR
CHALDAEA
Ur

Susa
ELAM
(Persian Gulf)

△ Mount Ararat

☐ Possible origin of semitic shepherds seeking cultivated regions in order to form permanent settlements

■ The "Fertile Crescent". Well-watered and easily cultivated land

⇦ Possible route of Terah and his son Abraham from Chaldaea in about 2000 BC

FROM SLAVERY TO THE PROMISED LAND

0 — 100 Miles

"Thy name shall not be called any more Jacob, but Israel . . . be fruitful and multiply; a nation and a company of nations shall be of thee, and kings shall come out of thy loins, and the land which I gave Abraham and Isaac, to thee I will give it."

THE LORD TO JACOB.   GENESIS 35, 11-12

◉ Cities in which Abraham, Isaac and Jacob lived in about 2000 BC. Abraham also settled for a while in Egypt

▲ Jacob's son Joseph sold into captivity and taken into Egypt

▨ Jewish settlement in Egypt from about 1800-1500 BC

◕ Cities built, for Pharoah, by Jewish forced labour

↑ Approximate route of the Jewish exodus, led by Moses, according to the biblical narrative

Succoth

Dothan ▲

Shechem ◉

Luz (Bethel) ◉ ◉ Ai
LAND OF Ephrath ◉
CANAAN
Mamre ◉ Hebron ◉
Gerar ◉

Beersheba ◉

Dead Sea

Armon

LAND OF MOAB

LAND OF EDOM
▲ Mount Hor

WILDERNESS OF ZIN

Kadesh Barnea

WILDERNESS OF PARAN

LAND OF MIDIAN

Etzion Geber

WILDERNESS OF SINAI

Rephidim

▲ Mount Sinai

WILDERNESS OF SIN

Makah

Elim

WILDERNESS OF SHUR

WILDERNESS OF ETHAM

Petusium

Raamses

LAND OF GOSHEN
Pithom ◕
Etham
Sukkot

Damietta

Rosetta

Sais

Heliopolis ●
E G Y P T
Memphis ●

Nile

"Behold the people of the children of Israel are more and mightier than we. Come on, let us deal wisely with them; lest they multiply, and it come to pass, that, when there falleth out any war, they join also unto our enemies, and fight against us, and so get them up out of the land."

"Therefore they did set over them taskmasters to afflict them with their burdens. And they built for Pharoah treasure cities, Pithom and Raamses. But the more they afflicted them, the more they multiplied and grew"

EXODUS 1, 9-12

2

ENTERING THE PROMISED LAND

"Ye shall drive out all the inhabitants before you...and ye shall dispossess the inhabitants of the land, and dwell therein...and ye shall divide the land by lot for an inheritance among your families"
GOD TO THE JEWS, NUMBERS 33,52-54

Sidon

Damascus

Tyre

PHOENICIANS

BASHAN

■ Non-Israelite tribes

➤ The Israelites led by Moses

⇨ The Israelites after the death of Moses

✚ Principal cities taken by siege

GILEAD

Edrei

Ramoth-gilead

"...utterly destroying the men, women and children of every city"
DEUTERONOMY 3-6

CANAANITES

Jordan

AMORITES

Ai

Jericho

Heshbon

AMMONITES

Ramoth-ammon

PHILISTINES

Ashdod

Ashkelon

Gaza

Mount Nebo

Death of Moses in sight of the promised land

JEBUSITES

MOABITES

AMALEKITES

River of Egypt

EDOMITES

MIDIANITES

"And they burnt all their cities wherein they dwelt, and all their goodly castles with fire"
NUMBERS 31-10

Ezion-geber

0   40
Miles

THE TWELVE TRIBES OF ISRAEL

"And I will send an Angel before them... unto a land flowing with milk and honey"

EXODUS 33, 2-3

SIDONIANS

△ Mount Lebanon

△ Mount Hermon

A R A M

ASHER

NAPHTALI

MAACHTHITES

GESHURITES

BASHAN

ARGOB

Mount △ Carmel

ZEBULON

△ Mount Tabor

ISSACHAR

Mount Gilboa △

Golan

MANASSEH

HAVOTH JAIR

MANASSEH

Mount Gerizim △ Shechem

Jordan

GAD

BASHAN

Ramoth Gilead

EPHRAIM

DAN

AMMONITES

BENJAMIN

REUBEN

PHILISTIA

SHEPHELA

JUDAH

Hebron

Bezer

SIMEON

MOABITES

The tribes of Israel

"Cities of refuge"

Other tribes and areas

EDOMITES

0   20
Miles

4

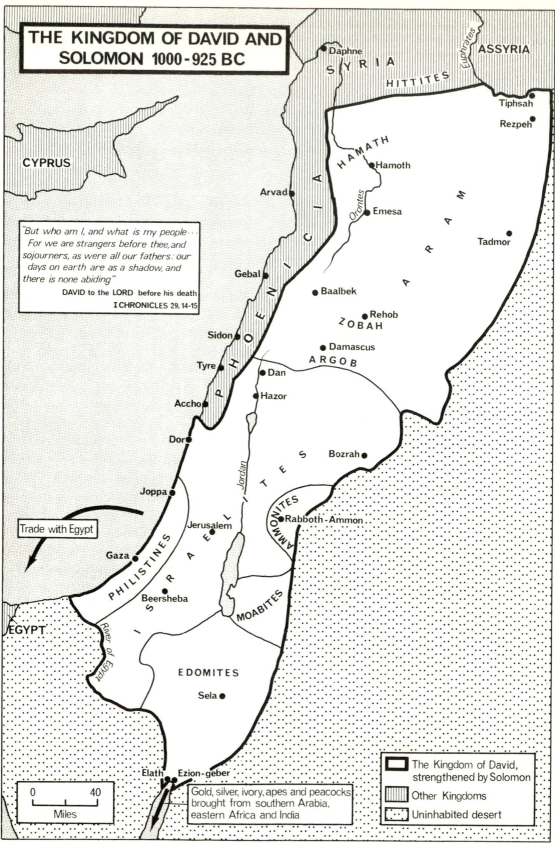

THE KINGDOM OF DAVID AND SOLOMON 1000-925 BC

ASSYRIA

Daphne

SYRIA

HITTITES

Euphrates

Tiphsah

Rezpeh

HAMATH

Hamoth

CYPRUS

Arvad

Orontes

Emesa

A R A M

Tadmor

"*But who am I, and what is my people...
For we are strangers before thee, and
sojourners, as were all our fathers: our
days on earth are as a shadow, and
there is none abiding*"

DAVID to the LORD before his death
I CHRONICLES 29, 14-15

Gebal

P H O E N I C I A

Baalbek

Rehob

Z O B A H

Sidon

Damascus

Tyre

A R G O B

Dan

Accho

Hazor

Dor

Bozrah

I S R A E L I T E S

Jordan

Joppa

A M M O N I T E S

Trade with Egypt

Jerusalem

Rabboth-Ammon

Gaza

P H I L I S T I N E S

Beersheba

M O A B I T E S

EGYPT

River of Egypt

E D O M I T E S

Sela

Elath   Ezion-geber

0	40
Miles	

Gold, silver, ivory, apes and peacocks
brought from southern Arabia,
eastern Africa and India

☐	The Kingdom of David, strengthened by Solomon
▥	Other Kingdoms
⸭	Uninhabited desert

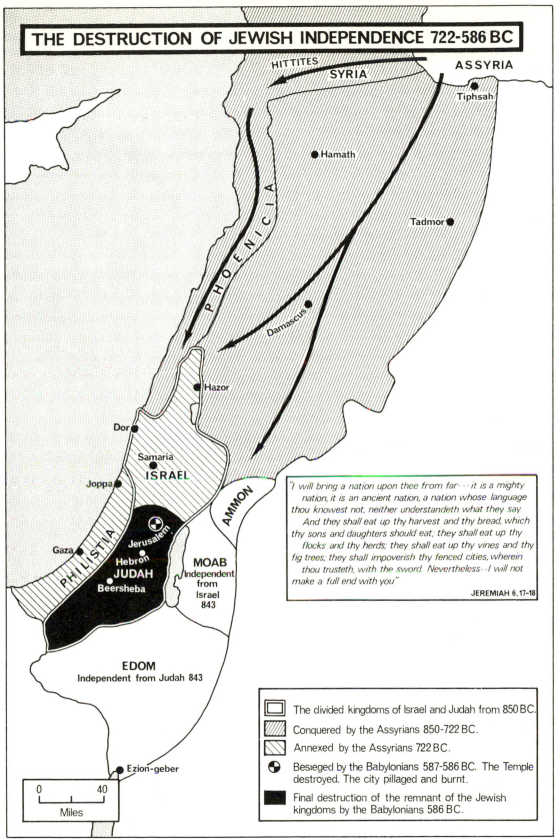

THE DESTRUCTION OF JEWISH INDEPENDENCE 722-586 BC

HITTITES

SYRIA

ASSYRIA

Tiphsah

Hamath

Tadmor

PHOENICIA

Damascus

Hazor

Dor

Samaria

ISRAEL

Joppa

AMMON

> "I will bring a nation upon thee from far···it is a mighty
> nation, it is an ancient nation, a nation whose language
> thou knowest not, neither understandeth what they say.
> And they shall eat up thy harvest and thy bread, which
> thy sons and daughters should eat; they shall eat up thy
> flocks and thy herds; they shall eat up thy vines and thy
> fig trees; they shall impoverish thy fenced cities, wherein
> thou trusteth, with the sword. Nevertheless···I will not
> make a full end with you"
>
> JEREMIAH 6, 17-18

Gaza

PHILISTIA

Jerusalem

Hebron

JUDAH

Beersheba

MOAB
Independent
from
Israel
843

EDOM
Independent from Judah 843

Ezion-geber

0   40
Miles

The divided kingdoms of Israel and Judah from 850 BC.

Conquered by the Assyrians 850-722 BC.

Annexed by the Assyrians 722 BC.

Besieged by the Babylonians 587-586 BC. The Temple
destroyed. The city pillaged and burnt.

Final destruction of the remnant of the Jewish
kingdoms by the Babylonians 586 BC.

THE FIRST DISPERSIONS
722-586 BC

Caspian Sea

CAUCASUS MTS.

△ Mount Ararat

● Hyrcania

● Nehavend

● Ecbatana

● Susiana

Persian Gulf

P E R S I A

● Mahoza
● Cutha
● Nippur
● Pumbedita
● Ellasar
● Sura
● Babylon

MESOPOTAMIA

Tigris

● Nineveh
● Resen
● Calah
● Ashur

● Sippara

● Ava

Euphrates

● Halah

● Haran
● Pethor

● Aleppo
● Tiphsah
● Rezeph

● Damascus

S Y R I A

● Caesarea

TAURUS MTS.

● Tarsus
CILICIA
● Seleuchia

● Antioch

◎ Jerusalem

● Aspendos

Mediterranean Sea

● Daphne

E G Y P T

Nile

● Alexandria

S I N A I

Red Sea

● Elephantine

● Syene

"Seek the peace of the city whither I have caused you to be carried away captives, and pray unto the Lord for it: for in the peace thereof shall ye have peace"
JEREMIAH 29·9

"By the rivers of Babylon, there we sat down; yea, we wept when we remembered Zion."
PSALM 137

"Ye walk every one after the imagination of his evil heart... Therefore will I cast you out of this land into a land that ye know not...where I will not shew you favour"
JEREMIAH 16, 12-13

→ Direction of the Jewish dispersions in 722 and 586 BC, following the Assyrian and Babylonian conquests

⇨ Direction of the Jewish dispersal after their revolt against Persia 359-338 BC

● Cities in which the Jews settled after their dispersal. The Jews quickly established vigorous intellectual and merchant communities throughout the "Diaspora" or area of their dispersal

100
0 Miles

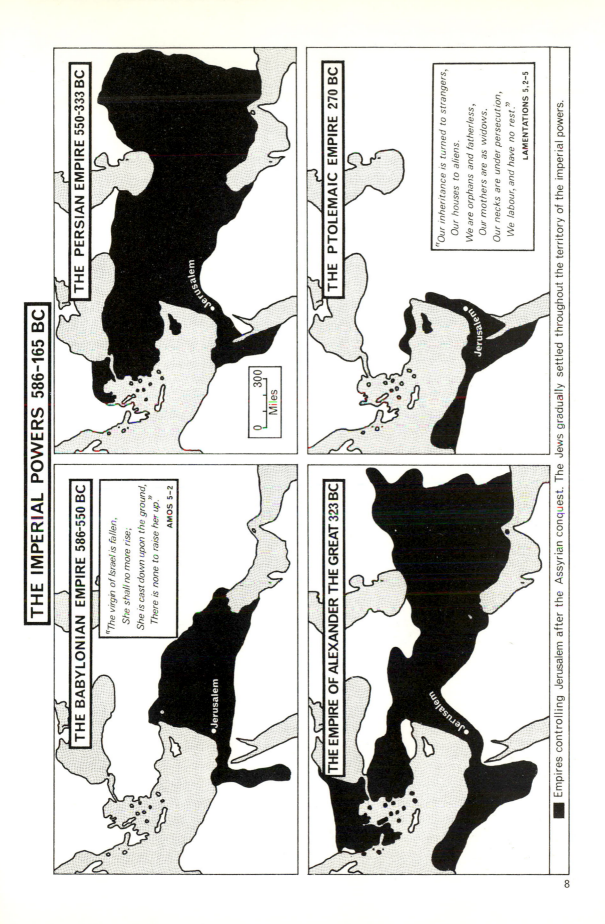

THE IMPERIAL POWERS 586–165 BC

THE BABYLONIAN EMPIRE 586–550 BC

"The virgin of Israel is fallen,
She shall no more rise;
She is cast down upon the ground,
There is none to raise her up."
AMOS 5–2

Jerusalem

THE PERSIAN EMPIRE 550–333 BC

Jerusalem

0 300
Miles

THE EMPIRE OF ALEXANDER THE GREAT 323 BC

Jerusalem

THE PTOLEMAIC EMPIRE 270 BC

Jerusalem

"Our inheritance is turned to strangers,
Our houses to aliens.
We are orphans and fatherless,
Our mothers are as widows.
Our necks are under persecution,
We labour, and have no rest."
LAMENTATIONS 5, 2–5

■ Empires controlling Jerusalem after the Assyrian conquest. The Jews gradually settled throughout the territory of the imperial powers.

8

THE JEWS OF THE EASTERN MEDITERRANEAN BOTH BEFORE AND AFTER THE ARAB CONQUEST

0   20
Miles

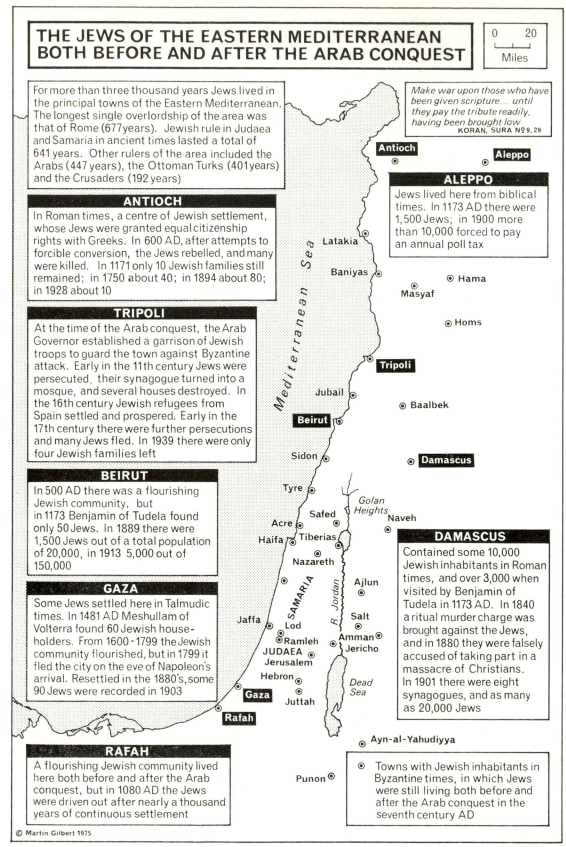

For more than three thousand years Jews lived in the principal towns of the Eastern Mediterranean. The longest single overlordship of the area was that of Rome (677 years). Jewish rule in Judaea and Samaria in ancient times lasted a total of 641 years. Other rulers of the area included the Arabs (447 years), the Ottoman Turks (401 years) and the Crusaders (192 years)

Make war upon those who have been given scripture... until they pay the tribute readily, having been brought low
KORAN, SURA No 9, 29

ANTIOCH

In Roman times, a centre of Jewish settlement, whose Jews were granted equal citizenship rights with Greeks. In 600 AD, after attempts to forcible conversion, the Jews rebelled, and many were killed. In 1171 only 10 Jewish families still remained; in 1750 about 40; in 1894 about 80; in 1928 about 10

ALEPPO

Jews lived here from biblical times. In 1173 AD there were 1,500 Jews; in 1900 more than 10,000 forced to pay an annual poll tax

TRIPOLI

At the time of the Arab conquest, the Arab Governor established a garrison of Jewish troops to guard the town against Byzantine attack. Early in the 11th century Jews were persecuted, their synagogue turned into a mosque, and several houses destroyed. In the 16th century Jewish refugees from Spain settled and prospered. Early in the 17th century there were further persecutions and many Jews fled. In 1939 there were only four Jewish families left

BEIRUT

In 500 AD there was a flourishing Jewish community, but in 1173 Benjamin of Tudela found only 50 Jews. In 1889 there were 1,500 Jews out of a total population of 20,000, in 1913 5,000 out of 150,000

DAMASCUS

Contained some 10,000 Jewish inhabitants in Roman times, and over 3,000 when visited by Benjamin of Tudela in 1173 AD. In 1840 a ritual murder charge was brought against the Jews, and in 1880 they were falsely accused of taking part in a massacre of Christians. In 1901 there were eight synagogues, and as many as 20,000 Jews

GAZA

Some Jews settled here in Talmudic times. In 1481 AD Meshullam of Volterra found 60 Jewish householders. From 1600-1799 the Jewish community flourished, but in 1799 it fled the city on the eve of Napoleon's arrival. Resettled in the 1880's, some 90 Jews were recorded in 1903

RAFAH

A flourishing Jewish community lived here both before and after the Arab conquest, but in 1080 AD the Jews were driven out after nearly a thousand years of continuous settlement

⊙ Towns with Jewish inhabitants in Byzantine times, in which Jews were still living both before and after the Arab conquest in the seventh century AD

© Martin Gilbert 1975

9

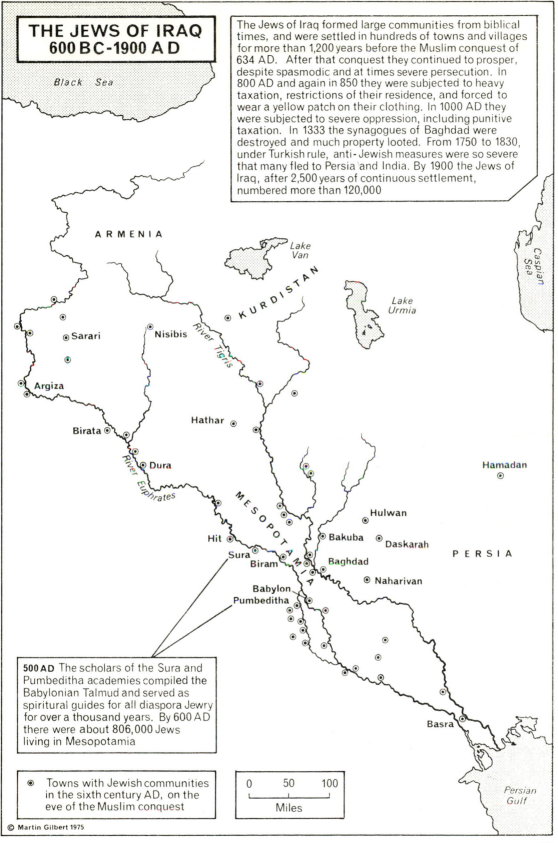

THE JEWS OF IRAQ
600 B C - 1900 A D

Black Sea

The Jews of Iraq formed large communities from biblical times, and were settled in hundreds of towns and villages for more than 1,200 years before the Muslim conquest of 634 AD. After that conquest they continued to prosper, despite spasmodic and at times severe persecution. In 800 AD and again in 850 they were subjected to heavy taxation, restrictions of their residence, and forced to wear a yellow patch on their clothing. In 1000 AD they were subjected to severe oppression, including punitive taxation. In 1333 the synagogues of Baghdad were destroyed and much property looted. From 1750 to 1830, under Turkish rule, anti-Jewish measures were so severe that many fled to Persia and India. By 1900 the Jews of Iraq, after 2,500 years of continuous settlement, numbered more than 120,000

ARMENIA

Lake Van

Caspian Sea

K U R D I S T A N

Lake Urmia

Sarari

Nisibis

River Tigris

Argiza

Hathar

Birata

River Euphrates

Dura

M E S O P O T A M I A

Hamadan

Hulwan

Hit

Bakuba   Daskarah

Sura

Biram   Baghdad   P E R S I A

Babylon   Naharivan

Pumbeditha

500 AD The scholars of the Sura and Pumbeditha academies compiled the Babylonian Talmud and served as spiritual guides for all diaspora Jewry for over a thousand years. By 600 AD there were about 806,000 Jews living in Mesopotamia

Basra

| ⊙ | Towns with Jewish communities in the sixth century AD, on the eve of the Muslim conquest |

0   50   100

Miles

Persian Gulf

© Martin Gilbert 1975

10

THE JEWS OF PERSIA 500 BC–1960 AD

Miles
0   200

KHORASAN

AZERBAIJAN

Caspian Sea

TABIRISTAN

KHUZISTAN

MAHOZA

Oxus

Tigris

Persian Gulf

Samarkand
Bukhara
Maimana
Merv
Herat
Tus
Meshed
Nishapur
Kerman
Kis
Muscat
Shiraz
Bushire
El Katif
Isfahan
Tustar
Ahwaz
Susa
Teheran
Rayy
Kashan
Nahawend
Hamadan
Kermanshah
Rudbar
Tabriz

1838 Entire Jewish community forcibly converted to Islam. As "Jedid-al-Islam" or "New Moslems" they continued practising Judaism secretly while outwardly devout Muslims

Jews not allowed to build the walls of their houses as high as those of their Muslim neighbours, or to ride on horseback in the streets

Independent Jewish Kingdom of Mahoza set up by Mar Zutra in 513 AD. In 520 Zutra was defeated by the Persians and he and his grandfather were then crucified

● Towns in which Benjamin of Tudela reported Jewish communities 1165-1173

◉ Other towns with Jewish communities

1948-1960. 55,000 Persian Jews returned to Israel 80,000 remain in Persia

801. Isaac, a Jew from Italy, returns to Europe with Abulabaz, a Persian elephant

Large Jewish community from 500 BC

1170. Centre of Jewish carpet trade. 15,000 Jews

"Usually compelled to live apart in a ghetto, they have from time immemorial suffered from disabilities of occupation, dress, and habits which have marked them out as social pariahs from their fellow creatures....As soon as any outburst of bigotry takes place in Persia the Jews are apt to be the first victims"

GEORGE CURZON in 1892

11

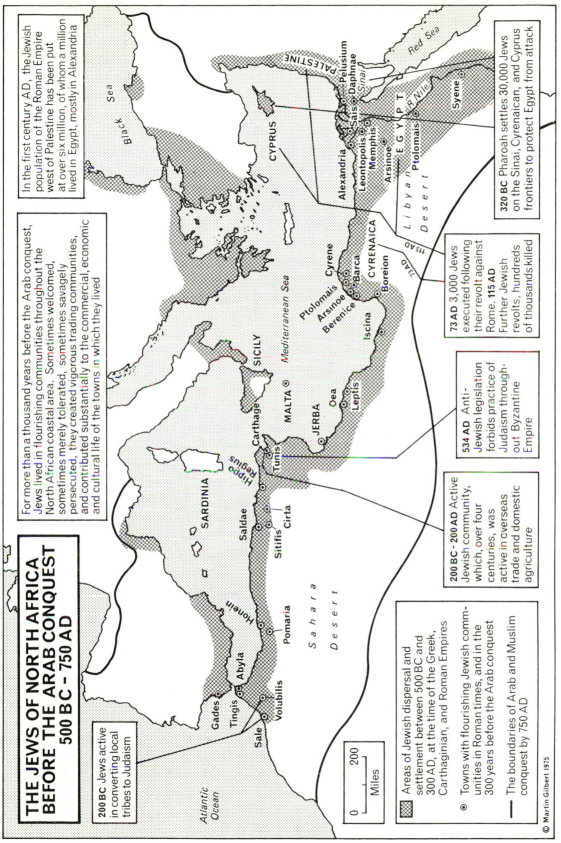

THE JEWS OF NORTH AFRICA BEFORE THE ARAB CONQUEST 500 BC – 750 AD

In the first century AD, the Jewish population of the Roman Empire west of Palestine has been put at over six million, of whom a million lived in Egypt, mostly in Alexandria

For more than a thousand years before the Arab conquest, Jews lived in flourishing communities throughout the North African coastal area. Sometimes welcomed, sometimes merely tolerated, sometimes savagely persecuted, they created vigorous trading communities, and contributed substantially to the commercial, economic and cultural life of the towns in which they lived

320 BC Pharoah settles 30,000 Jews on the Sinai, Cyrenaican, and Cyprus frontiers to protect Egypt from attack

73 AD 3,000 Jews executed following their revolt against Rome. **115 AD** Further Jewish revolts, hundreds of thousands killed

534 AD Anti-Jewish legislation forbids practice of Judaism throughout Byzantine Empire

200 BC – 200 AD Active Jewish community, which, over four centuries, was active in overseas trade and domestic agriculture

200 BC Jews active in converting local tribes to Judaism

Areas of Jewish dispersal and settlement between 500 BC and 300 AD, at the time of the Greek, Carthaginian, and Roman Empires

Towns with flourishing Jewish communities in Roman times, and in the 300 years before the Arab conquest

The boundaries of Arab and Muslim conquest by 750 AD

0   200
Miles

Atlantic Ocean

Sahara Desert

Libyan Desert

Mediterranean Sea

Black Sea

Red Sea

Nile

PALESTINE

Sinai

EGYPT

CYPRUS

CYRENAICA

SICILY

SARDINIA

MALTA

JERBA

Pelusium
Daphnae
Sais
Alexandria
Leontopolis
Memphis
Arsinoe
Ptolemais
Syene

Cyrene
Barca
Ptolemais
Arsinoe
Berenice
Boreion
Iscina
Leptis
Oea

Carthage
Tunis
Hippo Regius
Cirta
Saldae
Sitifis
Pomaria
Homein
Volubilis
Sale
Abyla
Tingis
Gades

115 AD
73 AD

© Martin Gilbert 1975

12

THE HASMONEAN JEWISH KINGDOM
165–63 BC

● Hasmonean towns and cities

▨ Judaising activity of Hasmoneans

✪ Unsuccessful sieges 100-96 B.C.

⟾ Invasion by Ptolemy repulsed after
an alliance between the Jews and
Egyptians in 100 B.C. The Egyptian
army which defeated Ptolemy was
commanded by two Jewish generals

◉ Cities conquered by the Hasmonean
King Alexander Jannai after 86 B.C.

Panaeas

65 B.C. Unsuccessful attack
on Damascus

Ptolemais (Acre)

Golan ◉

Migdal

Gamala ◉

Zippon

Gadara ◉

Amathus ◉

Dor

Skythopolis ◉

Pella ◉

Straton's Tower ◉

Apollonia ◉

Gerasa ◉

Jaffa

Gophna

Lod

Modiin

Yavne Yam

Dok

Yavne

Gezer

Free city of the Philistines
under an autonomous
government

Ashdod

Ashdod Yam

Jerusalem

Bethlehem

Medba ◉

63 B.C. Besieged by
Pompey for three
months. 12,000 Jews
massacred when the
Romans entered the
city. The priests, who
refused to interrupt
the service in the
Temple, were struck
down at the Altar

Ashkelon ✪

Hebron

Anthedon ◉

Gaza ◉

Raphia ◉

En Gedi ◉

Masada ◉

Beersheba

Ha Luza

IDUMEANS

165 Jewish revolt against Syrian rule
142 Syrians recognize Jewish independence
139 Roman Senate recognizes Jewish independence
130 Syrians besiege Jerusalem, but withdraw
96 Eight year civil war begins
83 Consolidation of the kingdom east of the Jordan
63 Conquest of the kingdom by the Romans

Jordan

0   20
Miles

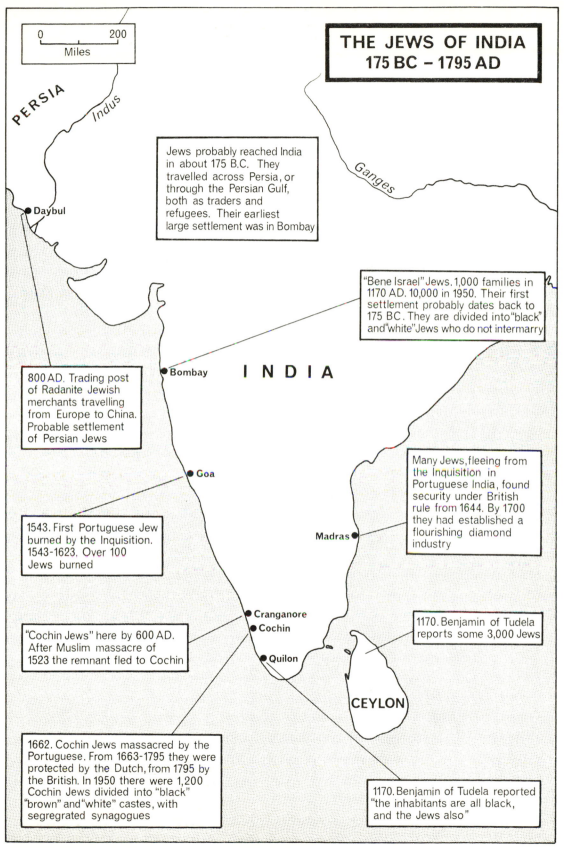

THE JEWS OF INDIA
175 BC – 1795 AD

0   200
Miles

PERSIA

Indus

Ganges

● Daybul

Jews probably reached India in about 175 B.C. They travelled across Persia, or through the Persian Gulf, both as traders and refugees. Their earliest large settlement was in Bombay

"Bene Israel" Jews. 1,000 families in 1170 AD. 10,000 in 1950. Their first settlement probably dates back to 175 BC. They are divided into "black" and "white" Jews who do not intermarry

800 AD. Trading post of Radanite Jewish merchants travelling from Europe to China. Probable settlement of Persian Jews

● Bombay   I N D I A

● Goa

Many Jews, fleeing from the Inquisition in Portuguese India, found security under British rule from 1644. By 1700 they had established a flourishing diamond industry

1543. First Portuguese Jew burned by the Inquisition. 1543-1623. Over 100 Jews burned

Madras ●

● Cranganore
● Cochin

1170. Benjamin of Tudela reports some 3,000 Jews

"Cochin Jews" here by 600 AD. After Muslim massacre of 1523 the remnant fled to Cochin

● Quilon

CEYLON

1662. Cochin Jews massacred by the Portuguese. From 1663-1795 they were protected by the Dutch, from 1795 by the British. In 1950 there were 1,200 Cochin Jews divided into "black" "brown" and "white" castes, with segregrated synagogues

1170. Benjamin of Tudela reported "the inhabitants are all black, and the Jews also"

14

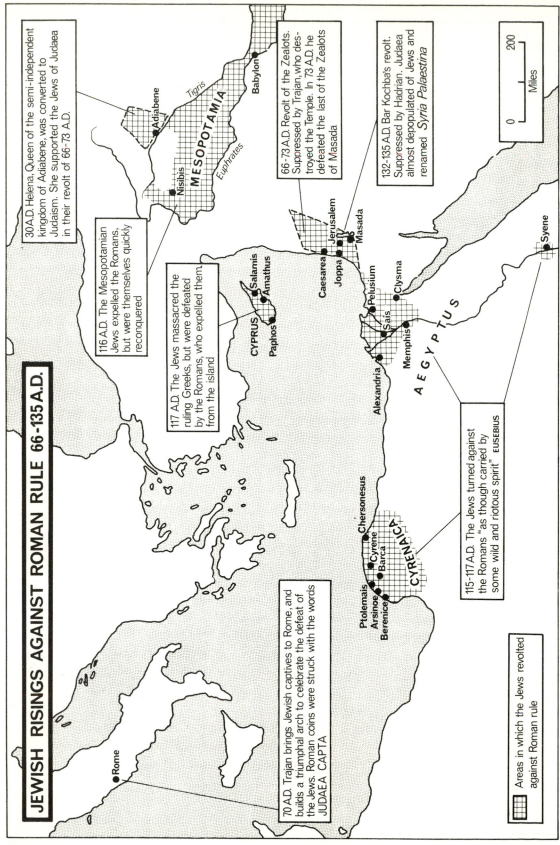

JEWISH RISINGS AGAINST ROMAN RULE 66-135 A.D.

30 A.D. Helena, Queen of the semi-independent kingdom of Adiabene, was converted to Judaism. She supported the Jews of Judaea in their revolt of 66-73 A.D.

116 A.D. The Mesopotamian Jews expelled the Romans, but were themselves quickly reconquered

117 A.D. The Jews massacred the ruling Greeks, but were defeated by the Romans, who expelled them from the island

66-73 A.D. Revolt of the Zealots. Suppressed by Trajan, who destroyed the Temple. In 73 A.D. he defeated the last of the Zealots of Masada

132-135 A.D. Bar Kochba's revolt. Suppressed by Hadrian. Judaea almost depopulated of Jews and renamed *Syria Palaestina*

70 A.D. Trajan brings Jewish captives to Rome, and builds a triumphal arch to celebrate the defeat of the Jews. Roman coins were struck with the words JUDAEA CAPTA

115-117 A.D. The Jews turned against the Romans "as though carried by some wild and riotous spirit" EUSEBIUS

Tigris

Euphrates

MESOPOTAMIA

Babylon

Adiabene

Nisibis

Jerusalem
Masada
Caesarea
Joppa
Pelusium
Clysma
Sais
Memphis
Alexandria

CYPRUS
Salamis
Amathus
Paphos

AEGYPTUS

Syene

Chersonesus
Cyrene
Barca
CYRENAICA
Ptolemais
Arsinoe
Berenice

Rome

Areas in which the Jews revolted against Roman rule

0   200
Miles

15

THE REVOLT OF THE ZEALOTS 66-73 AD

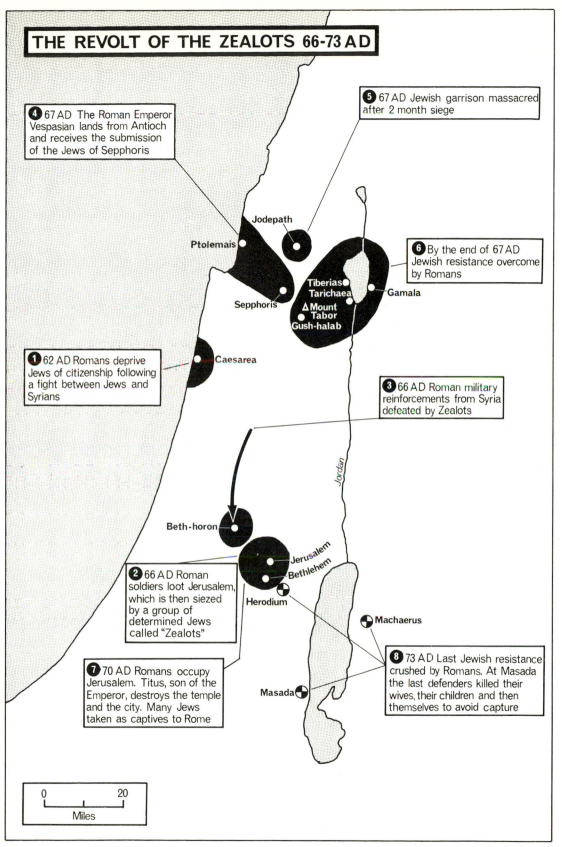

4 67 AD The Roman Emperor Vespasian lands from Antioch and receives the submission of the Jews of Sepphoris

5 67 AD Jewish garrison massacred after 2 month siege

6 By the end of 67 AD Jewish resistance overcome by Romans

1 62 AD Romans deprive Jews of citizenship following a fight between Jews and Syrians

3 66 AD Roman military reinforcements from Syria defeated by Zealots

2 66 AD Roman soldiers loot Jerusalem, which is then siezed by a group of determined Jews called "Zealots"

7 70 AD Romans occupy Jerusalem. Titus, son of the Emperor, destroys the temple and the city. Many Jews taken as captives to Rome

8 73 AD Last Jewish resistance crushed by Romans. At Masada the last defenders killed their wives, their children and then themselves to avoid capture

Jodepath

Ptolemais

Tiberias
Tarichaea
△ Mount Tabor
Gush-halab
Gamala

Sepphoris

Caesarea

Jordan

Beth-horon

Jerusalem
Bethlehem
Herodium

Machaerus

Masada

0   20
Miles

THE JEWS OF THE ROMAN EMPIRE 100-300 AD

GERMANIA

Colonia

Rhine

Regina

Aquincum

PANNONI

Lutetia

Genabum

Vesontio

Alps

Tergeste

Ravenna

DALMAT

GALLIA

Burdigala

Genua

ITALIA

Tolosa

Pyrenees

Massilia

APULIA

CALABR

HISPANIA

Roma

CAMPANIA

Corduba

SARDINIA

Gades

Caralis

Panormus

SICILIA

Volubilis

Carthago

Melite

Atlas

Mountains

Oea

Sahara Jews

S   A   H   A   R   A

Jews filled many occupations, being farmers and cattle raisers
(Mesopotamia), street traders (Egypt), slave-traders (Germany),
wine and olive-growers (Spain and North Africa), weavers,
garment-makers, actors, bakers and shipping-merchants
(Italy). They were equally active as agriculturalists and
town dwellers

By 300 A.D., the Jews had settled in every part of the Roman Empire except Britain. They were guaranteed freedom of religion and were allowed to practice Jewish law in disputes between Jews. They were exempt from military service.
There were probably at least three million Jews in 300 A.D., a million of whom lived west of Macedonia

0   200
Miles

Don

Tanais

Olbia

Phanagoria

Panticapaeum

Mountain Jews

Caucasus Mts.

Mursa

Danube

Serdica

MOESIA

Trapezus

Amisus

Byzantium

Prusa

ASSYRIA

Tigris

PHRYGIA

Ancyra

Melitene

MESOPOTAMIA

MACEDONIA

Tarsus

CILICIA

Ephesus

Sura

Euphrates

Delos

Pumbedita
Babylon

ACHAIA

LYCIA

CYPRUS

SYRIA

Damascus

Hierosolyma
(Jerusalem)

Cyrene

Berenice

Alexandria

Pelusium

Aelana

CYRENAICA

AEGYPTUS

Slave-dwelling
Jews

The 40,000 Jews of Cyprus were expelled after rebelling against Roman rule in 115 A.D.

■ Areas of widespread Jewish settlement

● Towns with large Jewish communities

◉ Isolated Jewish communities established after the Roman conquest of Palestine and surviving to this day

17

THE PREACHING OF ST. PAUL 45-57 A.D.

8 *"There is neither Jew nor Greek, there is neither bond nor free, there is neither male nor female: for ye are all one in Christ Jesus. And if ye be Christ's, then are ye Abraham's seed"*

PAUL to the GALATIANS

1 Birthplace of Saul, *"a Hebrew of Hebrews"* of the tribe of Benjamin, a Roman citizen later known as Paul

7 Paul imprisoned for two years; then sent to Rome where he was confined to his house for a further two years

ACTS 9-15

2 Paul persecuted Jews in Jerusalem for some years: *"He made a havoc of the church"*. Then, on the road to Damascus, he had a vision and was converted to Christianity. Jesus Christ said: *"He is a chosen vessel unto me, to bear my name before the children of Israel"*

ACTS 9-15

3 Paul expelled by the Jews

6 *"...he went into the synagogue and spake boldly for the space of three months, disputing and persuading"*

ACTS 19-9

4 *"...they received the word with all readiness of mind"*

ACTS 17-11

5 *"...he reasoned in the synagogue every sabbath and persuaded the Jews and the Greeks"*

ACTS 18-4

◐ Synagogues where Saul of Tarsus, known as Paul, preached Christianity to the Jews

◉ Other towns where Paul preached during his three missionary journeys

SYRIA

Damascus

Antioch
Seleucia

Ptolemais
Sidon
Tyre
Caesarea
Lydda
Jerusalem
Joppa

Tarsus

CILICIA

CYPRUS
Salamis
Paphos

PHRYGIA

Iconium
Lystra
Derbe

GALATIA

Dorylaeum

Antioch-in-Pisidia

PAMPHYLIA

Perga
Attalia
LYCIA
Patora
Myra

Ephesus
Miletus

MYSIA

LYDIA

Troas
Assos

THRACE

Samothrace

Philippi
Neapolis
Thessalonica
Beroea
MACEDONIA

ACHAIA
Athens
Corinth

100

0
Miles

JEWISH CONVERTS TO CHRISTIANITY 45-300 A.D.

Legend:
- ● Towns with large Jewish populations in which conversion to Christianity was widespread, 100-300 A.D.
- Areas of Jewish settlement in which Christianity had become the dominant religion by 300 A.D.
- ✝ The Seven Churches of Asia Minor

GREECE
Larissa
Thessalonica
Philippi
Delphi
Patrae
Corinth
Sparta
Phalara

ASIA MINOR
Nicomedia
Prusa
Assos
Mytelline
Samos
Cos
✝ Pergamum
✝ Thyatira
✝ Sardis
✝ Smyrna
✝ Philadelphia
Laodicea
✝ Ephesus
Halicarnassos
Rhodes
Ancyra
Iconium
Perga
Side
Olba
Tarsus
Sebaste

SYRIA
Antioch
Damascus
Bostra
Sidon
Tyre
Jerusalem
Caesarea

CYPRUS
Salamis
Citium
Soli

EGYPT
Pelusium
Alexandria

CRETE
Gnossos
Gortyna

CYRENAICA
Cyrene
Barca
Berenice

Miles
0   100

19

THE JEWS AND ISLAM 750 AD

Under Muslim rule the Jews found greater toleration than under Christianity. Thus the Jews of Toledo opened the gates of the city to welcome their Muslim liberators. There were nothing like the frequent massacres and expulsion which were the curse of Jews living in Christendom

0   400
Miles

The conquests of Islam by 750 AD

Cities with large Jewish communities

Principal areas of Jewish settlement

The two main trade routes from Baghdad to Samarkand: called the "Khorasan Road" along which Jews travelled and settled. It was also the overland route to China

Possible area of independent Jewish tribes, or Wild Jews, who fought successfully against Muslim domination

Indus

Daybul

Samarkand
Balkh
Maimana
Ghazni
Oxus
Herat
Merv
Tus
Bukhara
Kerman
Muscat
Khiva
Nishapur
Shiraz
Kis
Rayy
Hamadan
Baghdad Tustar
Nihawend
Ahwas
Zebid
Mocha
Tabriz
Kazvin
Mosul
Sura Basra
Kufa
Messene
Taima
Khaibar
Haran
Pumbedita
Tigris
Aleppo
Antioch
Ramleh
Euphrates
Damascus
Tyre
Fustat
Damietta
Aswan
Alexandria
Nile

Barca

SICILY

SARDINIA

Kairouan

Toledo
Cordova
Tlemcen

Cadiz
Fez

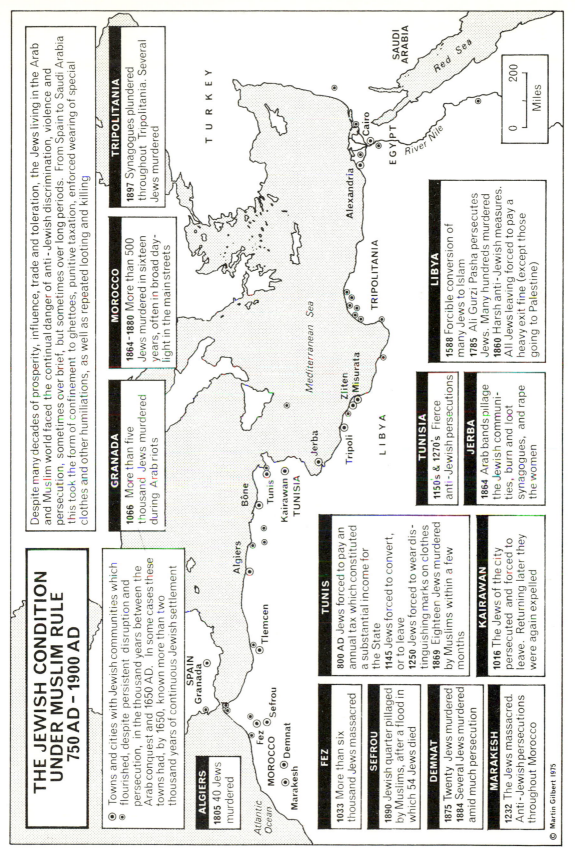

THE JEWISH CONDITION UNDER MUSLIM RULE 750 AD – 1900 AD

Despite many decades of prosperity, influence, trade and toleration, the Jews living in the Arab and Muslim world faced the continual danger of anti-Jewish discrimination, violence and persecution, sometimes over brief, but sometimes over long periods. From Spain to Saudi Arabia this took the form of confinement to ghettoes, punitive taxation, enforced wearing of special clothes and other humiliations, as well as repeated looting and killing

⊙ Towns and cities with Jewish communities which flourished, despite persistent disruption and persecution, in the thousand years between the Arab conquest and 1650 AD. In some cases these towns had, by 1650, known more than two thousand years of continuous Jewish settlement

ALGIERS
1805 40 Jews murdered

FEZ
1033 More than six thousand Jews massacred

SEFROU
1890 Jewish quarter pillaged by Muslims, after a flood in which 54 Jews died

DEMNAT
1875 Twenty Jews murdered
1884 Several Jews murdered amid much persecution

MARAKESH
1232 The Jews massacred. Anti-Jewish persecutions throughout Morocco

TUNIS
800 AD Jews forced to pay an annual tax which constituted a substantial income for the State
1145 Jews forced to convert, or to leave
1250 Jews forced to wear distinguishing marks on clothes
1869 Eighteen Jews murdered by Muslims within a few months

KAIRAWAN
1016 The Jews of the city persecuted and forced to leave. Returning later they were again expelled

GRANADA
1066 More than five thousand Jews murdered during Arab riots

MOROCCO
1864-1880 More than 500 Jews murdered in sixteen years, often in broad daylight in the main streets

TRIPOLITANIA
1897 Synagogues plundered throughout Tripolitania. Several Jews murdered

TUNISIA
1150's & 1270's Fierce anti-Jewish persecutions

JERBA
1864 Arab bands pillage the Jewish communities, burn and loot synagogues, and rape the women

LIBYA
1588 Forcible conversion of many Jews to Islam
1785 Ali Gurzi Pasha persecutes Jews. Many hundreds murdered
1860 Harsh anti-Jewish measures. All Jews leaving forced to pay a heavy exit fine (except those going to Palestine)

SAUDI ARABIA
Red Sea
TURKEY
Cairo
EGYPT
River Nile
Alexandria
Mediterranean Sea
TRIPOLITANIA
Jerba
Tripoli
Zliten
Misurata
LIBYA
Tunis
Bône
Kairawan
TUNISIA
Algiers
Tlemcen
SPAIN
Granada
Fez
Sefrou
MOROCCO
Demnat
Marakesh
Atlantic Ocean

0   200
Miles

© Martin Gilbert 1975

JEWISH TRADERS 800-900 A.D.

Jewish merchants played a leading part in trade after the fall of the Roman Empire.
A Persian writer in about 850 A.D. recorded the journeys of the Jewish traders known as "Radanites" who linked the Frankish and Chinese kingdoms by land and sea. Their name probably comes from a Persian phrase meaning "knowing the way"

0   800
Miles

The Great
Wall of China

Yu-chi

Kuang-chu

Chang-an

C H I N A
(Tang Dynasty)

TUGHUZGUR TURKS

Khotan

Kashgar

HIND
(INDIA)

Balkh

Sind

Calicut

Cranganore

GREAT BULGARIA

K H A Z A R I A

Burjan

Itil

Kerman

PERSIA

Al-Ubullah

Fars

Bagdad

Kufa

Jubba

Antioch

Oman

ARABIA

Damascus

Byzantium

Al-Jar

Jidda

Alexandria

Al-Farama (Pelusium)

Al-Qulzum (Suez)

Aachen

KINGDOM OF THE
FRANKS

Tangier

Sus-al-Aqsa

Kairouan

MAIN TRADE COMMODITIES
To China: Furs
               Beaver skins
               Swords
               Slave girls
               Eunuchs
From China: Cinnamon
               Spices
               Musk
               Camphor

● Principal trading cities

── Probable Radanite Jewish trade routes

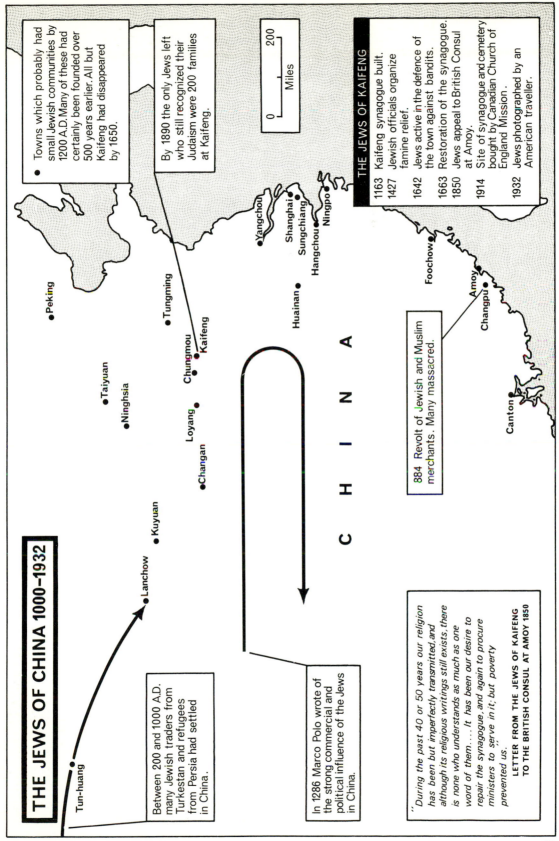

THE JEWS OF CHINA 1000–1932

- Towns which probably had small Jewish communities by 1200 A.D. Many of these had certainly been founded over 500 years earlier. All but Kaifeng had disappeared by 1650.

By 1890 the only Jews left who still recognized their Judaism were 200 families at Kaifeng.

THE JEWS OF KAIFENG

1163	Kaifeng synagogue built.
1427	Jewish officials organize famine relief.
1642	Jews active in the defence of the town against bandits.
1663	Restoration of the synagogue.
1850	Jews appeal to British Consul at Amoy.
1914	Site of synagogue and cemetery bought by Canadian Church of England Mission.
1932	Jews photographed by an American traveller.

0   200

Miles

Tun-huang

Lanchow

Kuyuan

Peking

Taiyuan

Ninghsia

Tungming

Loyang

Chungmou Kaifeng

Changan

Huainan

CHINA

Yangchou

Shanghai

Sungchiang

Hangchou

Ningpo

Foochow

Amoy

Changpu

Canton

884 Revolt of Jewish and Muslim merchants. Many massacred.

Between 200 and 1000 A.D. many Jewish traders from Turkestan and refugees from Persia had settled in China.

In 1286 Marco Polo wrote of the strong commercial and political influence of the Jews in China.

"During the past 40 or 50 years our religion has been but imperfectly transmitted, and although its religious writings still exists, there is none who understands as much as one word of them.... It has been our desire to repair the synagogue, and again to procure ministers to serve in it; but poverty prevented us."

LETTER FROM THE JEWS OF KAIFENG TO THE BRITISH CONSUL AT AMOY 1850

23

THE KHAZAR JEWISH KINGDOM 700-1016 AD

The Khazars were a heathen, nomad people from central Asia. In about 700 AD their king, Bulan, was converted to Judaism. A later king, Obadiah, greatly strengthened Judaism, inviting rabbis into his kingdom and building synagogues. The supreme court consisted of seven judges: 2 Jews, 2 Christians, 2 Muslims and a Heathen. Religious toleration was maintained for the kingdom's 300 years

HEATHENS

KHAZARIA

HEATHENS

Nishapur

Pumbedita

Sura

Trebizond

Constantinople

Alexandria

Cologne

Ravenna

Rome

Kairouan

Toulouse

Cordova

Fez

0   300

Miles

■ The Jewish kingdom of Khazaria at its widest extent

◉ Cities with large Jewish communities

Roman Catholics

Greek Catholics

Muslims

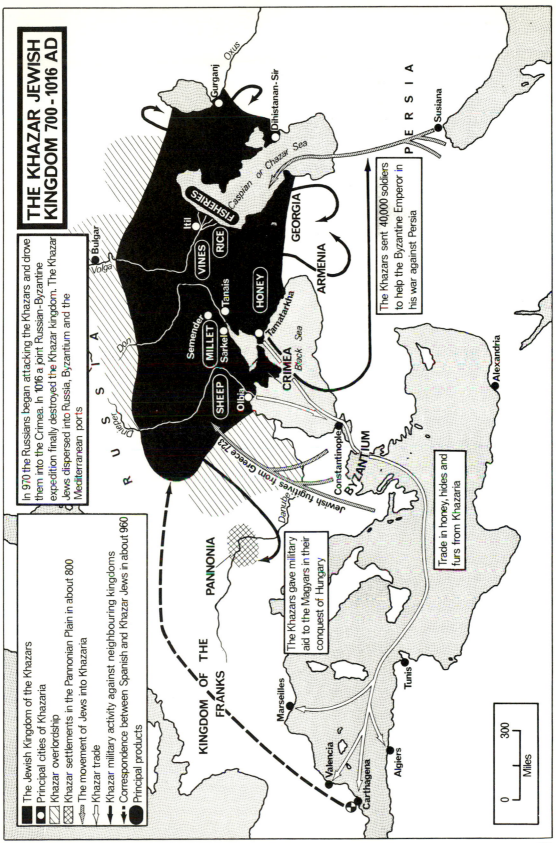

THE KHAZAR JEWISH KINGDOM 700 - 1016 AD

In 970 the Russians began attacking the Khazars and drove them into the Crimea. In 1016 a joint Russian-Byzantine expedition finally destroyed the Khazar kingdom. The Khazar Jews dispersed into Russia, Byzantium and the Mediterranean ports

The Khazars sent 40,000 soldiers to help the Byzantine Emperor in his war against Persia

Trade in honey, hides and furs from Khazaria

The Khazars gave military aid to the Magyars in their conquest of Hungary

■ The Jewish Kingdom of the Khazars
● Principal cities of Khazaria
▨ Khazar overlordship
▧ Khazar settlements in the Pannonian Plain in about 800
⟿ The movement of Jews into Khazaria
➡ Khazar trade
↓ Khazar military activity against neighbouring kingdoms
⇣ Correspondence between Spanish and Khazar Jews in about 960
◗ Principal products

Oxus

Gurganj

Dihistanan - Sir

PERSIA

Susiana

Caspian or Chazar Sea

FISHERIES

Itil

VINES

RICE

Bulgar

Volga

HONEY

GEORGIA

Tanais

ARMENIA

Tamatarkha

Don

Semender

MILLET

Sarkel

CRIMEA

Black Sea

SHEEP

Olbia

R U S S I A

Dnieper

Constantinople

BYZANTIUM

Jewish fugitives from Greece 723

Danube

PANNONIA

KINGDOM OF THE FRANKS

Alexandria

Marseilles

Valencia

Carthagena

Algiers

Tunis

0   300
Miles

THE JEWS OF BYZANTIUM 640–1532

0 — 200 Miles

700-1000 . Constant exodus of Jewish refugees to Khazaria

1096. Jews trading in Christian slaves

692. The Council forbids Christians to use Jewish doctors. Intermarriage becomes punishable by death. No new synagogues must be built. Jews could not own Christian slaves

1320. Jews forced to wear a yellow badge

1028. Jews siezed by Muslim pirates and ransomed to the Jews of Cairo and Alexandria

640 Heraclius orders forcible conversions
721 Leo III orders baptism for all Jews and Muslims
873 Basil I forbids practice of Judaism
930 Romanos I encourages baptism of Jews

c.1170. Benjamin of Tudela wrote of the Wallachians "They call the Jews their brethren. When they happen to meet them they rob them, but refrain from killing them as they kill the Greeks"

1480. Jews played an important part in defending Rhodes against Turks.
1502. All Jews were forcibly converted, expelled or taken into slavery

c.1300. Jews exported salt and imported textiles

1532. Genoese pirates sieze Jews in order to sell them into slavery

1430. Catalan pirates sieze Jews for ransom in Spain

Tephrice

Antioch

CYPRUS

CRIMEA

Kaffa

Kherson

Nicaea

Attalia

Rhodes

Alexandria

Cairo

EGYPT

Danube

BULGARIA

Constantinople

Gallipoli
Abydos
Smyrna
Ephesus
Kastoria
Mastaura
Patras
Modon
Durazzo
Corfu

― The boundaries of Byzantium in 1180
◉ Principal Ghettoes
▨ Areas of thick Jewish settlement
• Towns with large Jewish communities

26

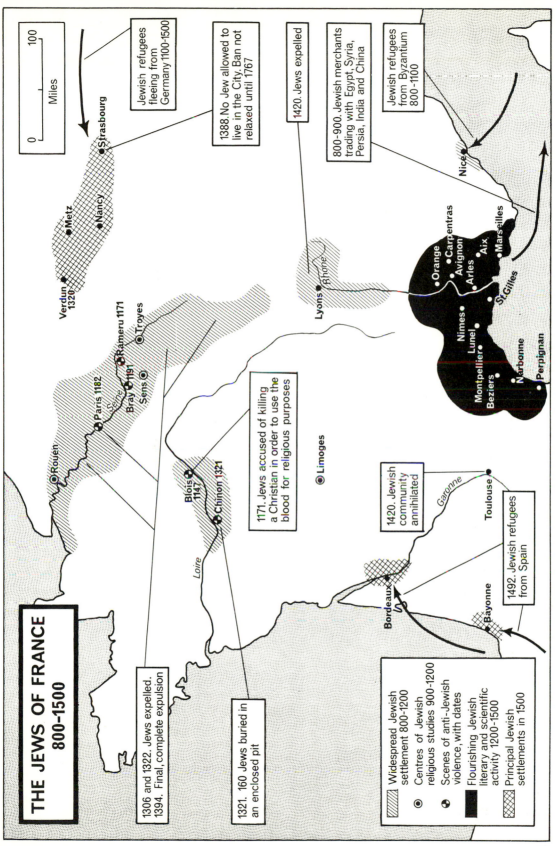

THE JEWS OF FRANCE 800-1500

Jewish refugees fleeing from Germany 1100-1500

1388. No Jew allowed to live in the City. Ban not relaxed until 1767

1420. Jews expelled

800-900. Jewish merchants trading with Egypt, Syria, Persia, India and China

Jewish refugees from Byzantium 800-1100

1171. Jews accused of killing a Christian in order to use the blood for religious purposes

1420. Jewish community annihilated

1492. Jewish refugees from Spain

1306 and 1322. Jews expelled. 1394. Final, complete expulsion

1321. 160 Jews buried in an enclosed pit

Strasbourg

Metz
Nancy

Verdun 1320

Paris 1182
Bray 1191
Sens
Ramerupt 1171
Troyes

Rouen

Blois 1147
Chinon 1321

Limoges

Lyons

Rhône

Orange
Carpentras
Avignon
Arles
Aix
Marseilles
Nîmes
St-Gilles
Lunel
Montpellier
Béziers
Narbonne
Perpignan

Nice

Garonne
Toulouse
Bordeaux
Bayonne

Loire
Seine

Miles
0   100

Widespread Jewish settlement 800-1200

Centres of Jewish religious studies 900-1200

Scenes of anti-Jewish violence, with dates

Flourishing Jewish literary and scientific activity 1200-1500

Principal Jewish settlements in 1500

THE JEWS OF ARABIA, 722 BC - 1948 AD

0 miles 200
0 kilometres 400

The first Jews to settle in Arabia did so after the Assyrian conquests of 722 BC, followed by further Jews who fled after the Babylonian destruction of the Temple in Jerusalem in 586 BC. Jews are mentioned in Babylonian inscriptions of 555 to 539 BC in Tayma and Yathrib. An inscription of 355 BC in Dedan refers to a Jewish family, as does another inscription in al-Hijr. By the time of Mohammed many Jewish poets were known in Arabia, among them Samuel 'King' of Tayma. Only after Mohammed's hopes of converting the Jews of Medina to Islam were disappointed did his relations with them deteriorate

From 644 AD Jews began to be expelled from the Hedjaz by Muslim rulers. Most fled to the Yemen, where about 55,000 Jews were living in 1948

Jews leaving southern Arabia in search of trade or refuge may have been the first 'Ethiopian' Jews

© Martin Gilbert 1985

Mediterranean Sea

Jerusalem

I R A Q

Tigris

Euphrates

(ASSYRIA, BABYLONIA)

Persian Gulf

E G Y P T

Sinai

Nile

Red Sea

H E D J A Z

Maqna

Mada'in Salih (al-Hijr)
al-Ula (Dedan)

Tayma
Fadak
Yadia
Khaybar
Yathrib

A R A B I A

Mecca
al-Ta'if

S U D A N

ETHIOPIA

Najran
H I M Y A R
Sana
Zafar
Zabid
S A B A (YEMEN)
Kinda
Aden

28

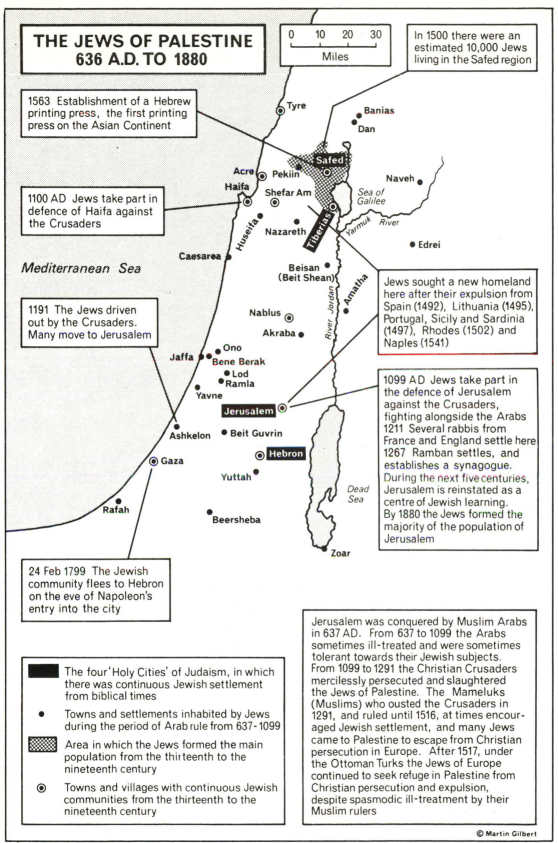

THE JEWS OF PALESTINE 636 A.D. TO 1880

0 10 20 30
Miles

In 1500 there were an estimated 10,000 Jews living in the Safed region

1563 Establishment of a Hebrew printing press, the first printing press on the Asian Continent

1100 AD Jews take part in defence of Haifa against the Crusaders

1191 The Jews driven out by the Crusaders. Many move to Jerusalem

Mediterranean Sea

Jews sought a new homeland here after their expulsion from Spain (1492), Lithuania (1495), Portugal, Sicily and Sardinia (1497), Rhodes (1502) and Naples (1541)

1099 AD Jews take part in the defence of Jerusalem against the Crusaders, fighting alongside the Arabs 1211 Several rabbis from France and England settle here 1267 Ramban settles, and establishes a synagogue. During the next five centuries, Jerusalem is reinstated as a centre of Jewish learning. By 1880 the Jews formed the majority of the population of Jerusalem

24 Feb 1799 The Jewish community flees to Hebron on the eve of Napoleon's entry into the city

Tyre

Banias
Dan

Safed
Acre
Haifa
Pekiin
Naveh
Shefar Am
Sea of Galilee
Huseifa
Nazareth
Tiberias
Yarmuk River
Caesarea
Edrei
Beisan (Beit Shean)
River Jordan
Amatha
Nablus
Akraba
Ono
Jaffa
Bene Berak
Lod
Ramla
Yavne
Jerusalem
Ashkelon
Beit Guvrin
Hebron
Gaza
Yuttah
Dead Sea
Rafah
Beersheba
Zoar

Jerusalem was conquered by Muslim Arabs in 637 AD. From 637 to 1099 the Arabs sometimes ill-treated and were sometimes tolerant towards their Jewish subjects. From 1099 to 1291 the Christian Crusaders mercilessly persecuted and slaughtered the Jews of Palestine. The Mameluks (Muslims) who ousted the Crusaders in 1291, and ruled until 1516, at times encouraged Jewish settlement, and many Jews came to Palestine to escape from Christian persecution in Europe. After 1517, under the Ottoman Turks the Jews of Europe continued to seek refuge in Palestine from Christian persecution and expulsion, despite spasmodic ill-treatment by their Muslim rulers

- ▬ The four 'Holy Cities' of Judaism, in which there was continuous Jewish settlement from biblical times
- ● Towns and settlements inhabited by Jews during the period of Arab rule from 637-1099
- ▨ Area in which the Jews formed the main population from the thirteenth to the nineteenth century
- ◉ Towns and villages with continuous Jewish communities from the thirteenth to the nineteenth century

© Martin Gilbert

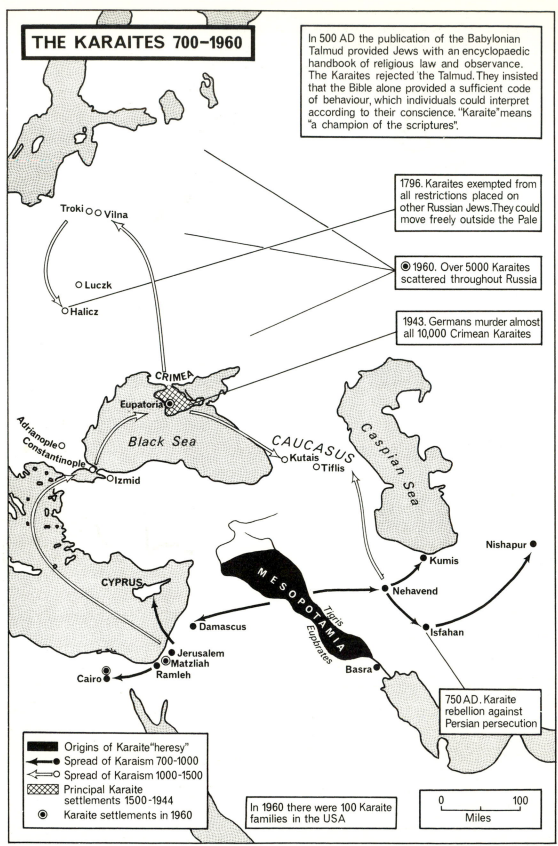

THE KARAITES 700–1960

In 500 AD the publication of the Babylonian Talmud provided Jews with an encyclopaedic handbook of religious law and observance. The Karaites rejected the Talmud. They insisted that the Bible alone provided a sufficient code of behaviour, which individuals could interpret according to their conscience. "Karaite" means "a champion of the scriptures".

1796. Karaites exempted from all restrictions placed on other Russian Jews. They could move freely outside the Pale

1960. Over 5000 Karaites scattered throughout Russia

1943. Germans murder almost all 10,000 Crimean Karaites

Troki ○○ Vilna

○ Luczk

○ Halicz

CRIMEA

Eupatoria ◉

Adrianople ○
Constantinople ○
○ Izmid

Black Sea

CAUCASUS
○ Kutais
○ Tiflis

Caspian Sea

Nishapur ●

● Kumis

CYPRUS

● Nehavend

● Isfahan

MESOPOTAMIA

Tigris

Euphrates

● Damascus

Jerusalem
◉ Matzliah
Cairo ◎   Ramleh

Basra ●

750 AD. Karaite rebellion against Persian persecution

Legend:

■	Origins of Karaite "heresy"
◄—●	Spread of Karaism 700–1000
◁—○	Spread of Karaism 1000–1500
▨	Principal Karaite settlements 1500–1944
◉	Karaite settlements in 1960

In 1960 there were 100 Karaite families in the USA

```
0          100
     Miles
```

THE JEWS OF GERMANY 500–1000

Baltic Sea

North Sea

Elbe

BOHEMIA

Rhine

Meuse

◉ Magdeburg

◉ Merseburg

◉ Cologne

F
R
A
N
C
E

Moselle

Mainz ◉   ◉ Frankfurt

◉ Verdun   Worms ◉   ◉ Würzburg   Prague ◉

◉ Metz   Speyer ◉

Ratisbon ◉

Danube

◉ Augsburg

St.Gothard Pass

Brenner Pass

Loebl Pass

HUNGARY

Rhone Valley

Venice ◉

Pola ●

● Avignon   ● Genoa

Ravenna ●

● Marseille

● Livorno

Adriatic Sea

● Rome

Mediterranean Sea

●	Centres of Jewish settlement in about 500. These settlements had all been founded in Roman times
←	Jewish migration northward across the Alps 500–1000
▬	The German Empire in 1000 AD
～	Rivers along whose valleys Jews settled as traders. Most towns had small Jewish communities by 1000
◉	Principal Jewish communities in Germany by 1000

0   100
Miles

THE JEWS OF CENTRAL EUROPE 1000–1500

1266. Church Council decreed that "Jews...shall not live side by side with the Christians, but shall live apart in houses adjoining each other in some section of the city or village. The section inhabited by Jews shall be separated from the Christian dwelling-place by a hedge, wall or ditch

1279. Church Council decreed that all Jews must wear a ring of red cloth on the left hand side of their outer garments

LITHUANIA

POLAND

OTTOMAN EMPIRE

Danube

Budapest 1348 1360

1348,1360

1364

HUNGARY

1349

Vienna 1349 1364 1420

AUSTRIA

Oder

Breslau 1349

SILESIA

Görlitz

Zittau

Bautzen

1389. 300 killed
1541. Expulsion

BOHEMIA

Prague

1421

1421

Passau

1401.48 burnt to death

Görz
Udine Görz Trieste

Pola

ISTRIA

VENETIA

Venice

BRANDENBURG

Berlin 1349,1510,1571

Magdeburg

1213

SAXONY

Meissen

Halle

Leipzig

Dresden

Plauen

1543

Regensberg

BAVARIA

Munich

Augsburg

Elbe

Hamburg

Nordhausen

1205

Erfurt
1212 Gotha 1215

Bamberg

Nuremberg

Fürth

1330's

Ulm

1330's

Schaffhausen 1299

Wintertur 1294 St.Gallen 1268

Zurich 1299

Lucerne 1299

1096, 1100–1400

1096, 1100–1400

Frankfurt

1012, 1096

Rhine

Mainz
1096

Worms

Speyer

RHINELAND

Cologne

Trier

Metz

HOLLAND

Amsterdam

Rhine

From Portugal 1497

From Spain 1492

Basel

Aargau

SWITZERLAND

Neuchatel

Solothurn

1259 Berne

ALSACE

1330's

● Towns with colleges for Jewish studies by 1500

● Principal Jewish communities

█ Towns where the Jews were attacked with violence or expelled

↓ The flight of Jews from persecution or following expulsion, with dates

Miles
0   100

32

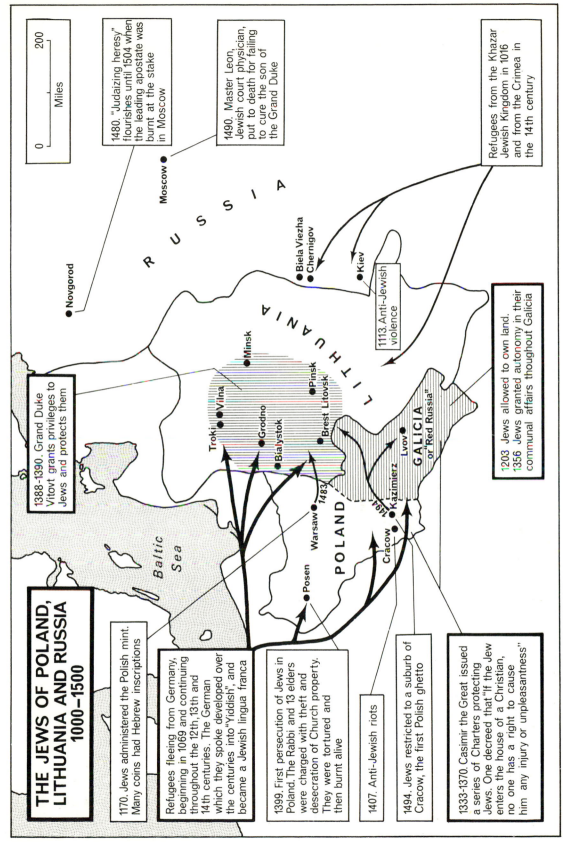

THE JEWS OF POLAND, LITHUANIA AND RUSSIA 1000–1500

Scale: 0 — 200 Miles

1480. "Judaizing heresy" flourishes until 1504 when the leading apostate was burnt at the stake in Moscow

1490. Master Leon, Jewish court physician, put to death for failing to cure the son of the Grand Duke

Refugees from the Khazar Jewish Kingdom in 1016 and from the Crimea in the 14th century

1388–1390. Grand Duke Vitovt grants privileges to Jews and protects them

1203 Jews allowed to own land.
1356 Jews granted autonomy in their communal affairs thoughout Galicia

1113. Anti-Jewish violence

1170. Jews administered the Polish mint. Many coins had Hebrew inscriptions

Refugees fleeing from Germany, beginning in 1069 and continuing throughout the 12th, 13th and 14th centuries. The German which they spoke developed over the centuries into "Yiddish", and became a Jewish lingua franca

1399. First persecution of Jews in Poland. The Rabbi and 13 elders were charged with theft and desecration of Church property. They were tortured and then burnt alive

1407. Anti-Jewish riots

1494. Jews restricted to a suburb of Cracow, the first Polish ghetto

1333-1370. Casimir the Great issued a series of Charters protecting Jews. One decreed that "If the Jew enters the house of a Christian, no one has a right to cause him any injury or unpleasantness"

Moscow

R U S S I A

Novgorod

Biela Viezha
Chernigov

Kiev

L I T H U A N I A

Minsk

Troki • Vilna

Grodno

Białystok

Pinsk

Brest Litovsk

Posen

Warsaw

P O L A N D

1483

Cracow

Kazimierz

1494

GALICIA or "Red Russia"

Lvov

Baltic Sea

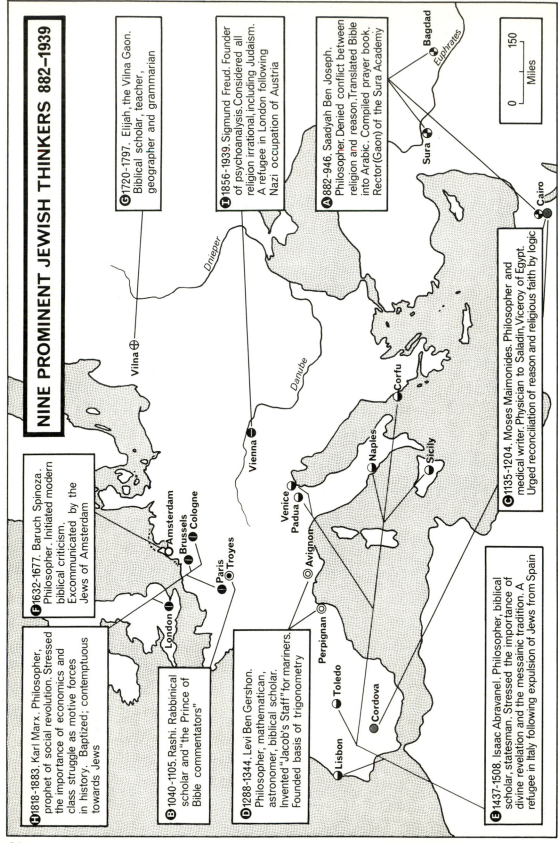

NINE PROMINENT JEWISH THINKERS 882–1939

G 1720-1797. Elijah, the Vilna Gaon. Biblical scholar, teacher, geographer and grammarian

H 1856-1939. Sigmund Freud. Founder of psychoanalysis. Considered all religion irrational, including Judaism. A refugee in London following Nazi occupation of Austria

A 882-946. Saadyah Ben Joseph. Philosopher. Denied conflict between religion and reason. Translated Bible into Arabic. Compiled prayer book. Rector (Gaon) of the Sura Academy

C 1135-1204. Moses Maimonides. Philosopher and medical writer. Physician to Saladin, Viceroy of Egypt. Urged reconciliation of reason and religious faith by logic

I 1818-1883. Karl Marx. Philosopher, prophet of social revolution. Stressed the importance of economics and class struggle as motive forces in history. Baptized; contemptuous towards Jews

F 1632-1677. Baruch Spinoza. Philosopher. Initiated modern biblical criticism. Excommunicated by the Jews of Amsterdam

B 1040-1105. Rashi. Rabbinical scholar and "the Prince of Bible commentators"

D 1288-1344. Levi Ben Gershon. Philosopher, mathematician, astronomer, biblical scholar. Invented "Jacob's Staff" for mariners. Founded basis of trigonometry

E 1437-1508. Isaac Abravanel. Philosopher, biblical scholar, statesman. Stressed the importance of divine revelation and the messainic tradition. A refugee in Italy following expulsion of Jews from Spain

Bagdad

Euphrates

0   150
Miles

Sura

Cairo

Dnieper

Danube

Vilna

Vienna

Corfu

Naples

Sicily

Amsterdam
Brussels
Cologne
London
Paris
Troyes

Venice
Padua
Avignon

Perpignan

Toledo
Lisbon
Cordova

34

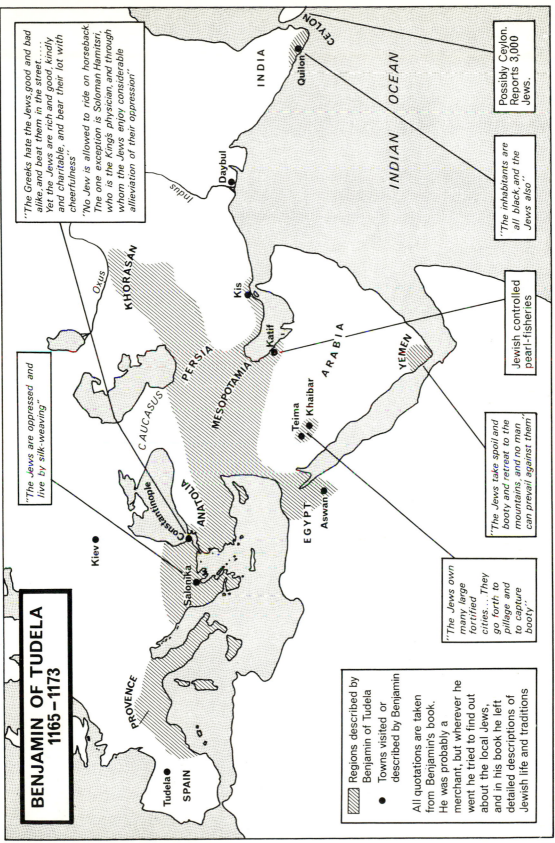

BENJAMIN OF TUDELA 1165–1173

SPAIN
● Tudela

PROVENCE

● Kiev

● Salonika

CONSTANTINOPLE

ANATOLIA

CAUCASUS

KHORASAN

Oxus

PERSIA

MESOPOTAMIA

● Kis

● Katif

EGYPT
Aswan ●

ARABIA

Teima ●
Khaibar ●

YEMEN

Indus

Daybul ●

INDIA

Quilon ●

CEYLON

INDIAN OCEAN

"The Greeks hate the Jews, good and bad alike, and beat them in the street....... Yet the Jews are rich and good, kindly and charitable, and bear their lot with cheerfulness"

"No Jew is allowed to ride on horseback. The one exception is Soloman Hamitsri, who is the King's physician, and through whom the Jews enjoy considerable allieviation of their oppression"

"The Jews are oppressed and live by silk-weaving"

"The Jews own many large fortified cities....They go forth to pillage and to capture booty"

"The Jews take spoil and booty and retreat to the mountains, and no man can prevail against them"

Jewish controlled pearl-fisheries

"The inhabitants are all black, and the Jews also"

Possibly Ceylon. Reports 3,000 Jews.

Regions described by Benjamin of Tudela

● Towns visited or described by Benjamin

All quotations are taken from Benjamin's book. He was probably a merchant, but wherever he went he tried to find out about the local Jews, and in his book he left detailed descriptions of Jewish life and traditions

35

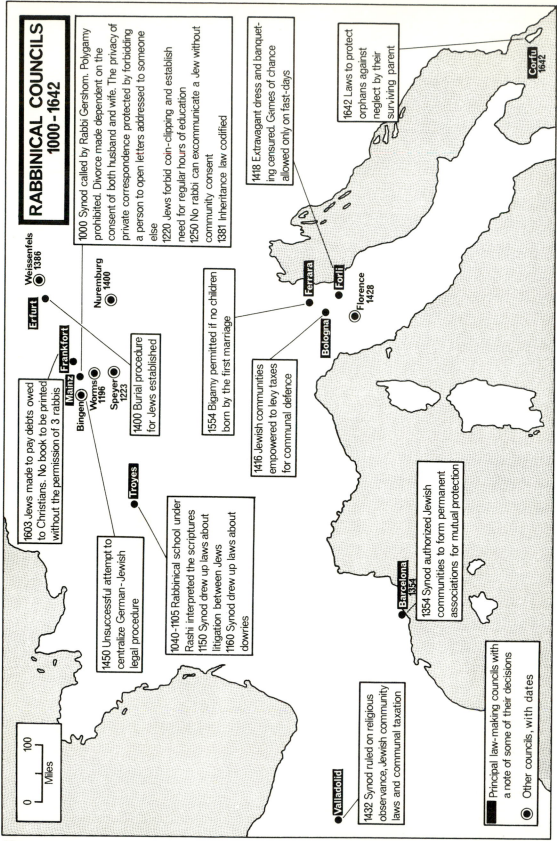

RABBINICAL COUNCILS
1000–1642

1000 Synod called by Rabbi Gershom. Polygamy prohibited. Divorce made dependent on the consent of both husband and wife. The privacy of private correspondence protected by forbidding a person to open letters addressed to someone else

1220 Jews forbid coin-clipping and establish need for regular hours of education

1250 No rabbi can excommunicate a Jew without community consent

1381 Inheritance law codified

1418 Extravagant dress and banqueting censured. Games of chance allowed only on fast-days

1642 Laws to protect orphans against neglect by their surviving parent

Corfu 1642

Weissenfels ● 1386

Erfurt

Nuremburg ● 1400

Frankfort

Mainz

Bingen ●
Worms ● 1196
Speyer ● 1223

1400 Burial procedure for Jews established

Ferrara

Forli

● Florence 1428

Bologna

1416 Jewish communities empowered to levy taxes for communal defence

1554 Bigamy permitted if no children born by the first marriage

1603 Jews made to pay debts owed to Christians. No book to be printed without the permission of 3 rabbis

1450 Unsuccessful attempt to centralize German-Jewish legal procedure

Troyes

1040-1105 Rabbinical school under Rashi interpreted the scriptures
1150 Synod drew up laws about litigation between Jews
1160 Synod drew up laws about dowries

Barcelona 1354

1354 Synod authorized Jewish communities to form permanent associations for mutual protection

● **Valladolid**

1432 Synod ruled on religious observance, Jewish community laws and communal taxation

0 ___ 100
Miles

▬ Principal law-making councils with a note of some of their decisions

◉ Other councils, with dates

36

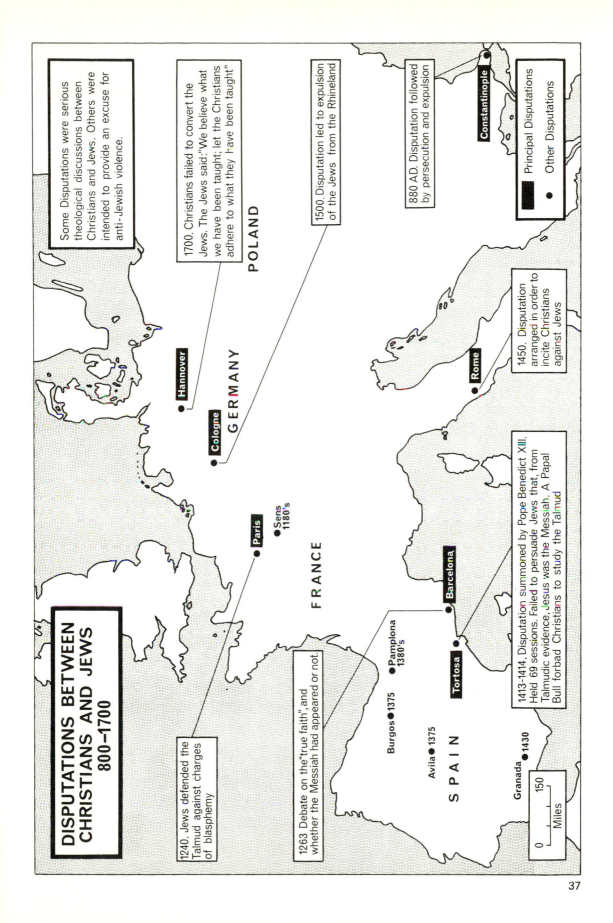

DISPUTATIONS BETWEEN CHRISTIANS AND JEWS 800–1700

Some Disputations were serious theological discussions between Christians and Jews. Others were intended to provide an excuse for anti-Jewish violence.

1700. Christians failed to convert the Jews. The Jews said:"We believe what we have been taught; let the Christians adhere to what they have been taught"

1500. Disputation led to expulsion of the Jews from the Rhineland

880 AD. Disputation followed by persecution and expulsion

1450. Disputation arranged in order to incite Christians against Jews

1413-1414. Disputation summoned by Pope Benedict XIII. Held 69 sessions. Failed to persuade Jews that, from Talmudic evidence, Jesus was the Messiah. A Papal Bull forbad Christians to study the Talmud

1240. Jews defended the Talmud against charges of blasphemy.

1263 Debate on the"true faith", and whether the Messiah had appeared or not.

■ Principal Disputations
● Other Disputations

POLAND

GERMANY

■ Hannover
■ Cologne

■ Paris
●Sens
1180's

FRANCE

■ Constantinople

■ Rome

SPAIN

Burgos●1375
●Pamplona
1380's
Avila●1375
■ Tortosa
■ Barcelona
Granada●1430

0   150
Miles

THE GERMAN CRUSADE 1096

POLAND

Pest

40

0   Miles

Nitra

Vienna

Wieselburg

H U N G A R Y

Stuhlweissenburg

M O R A V I A

Prague

B O H E M I A

A U S T R I A

Danube

Ratisbon

10,000 Crusaders under Volkmar

Remnant of Count Emich's band

12,000 Crusaders under Gottschalk

B A V A R I A

Wevelinghofen

Mainz

Worms

Speyer

Rhine

Eller

Xanten

Neuss

Cologne

Trier

Metz

15,000 Crusaders under Count Emich of Leisingen

Route of crusaders under Emich on their way to Jerusalem

Route of other crusaders 1096

Towns in which the crusaders massacred the Jews

Towns in which the local Archbishop and clergy interceded to protect the Jews, often in vain

Towns in which the crusaders were themselves massacred by the Hungarians

38

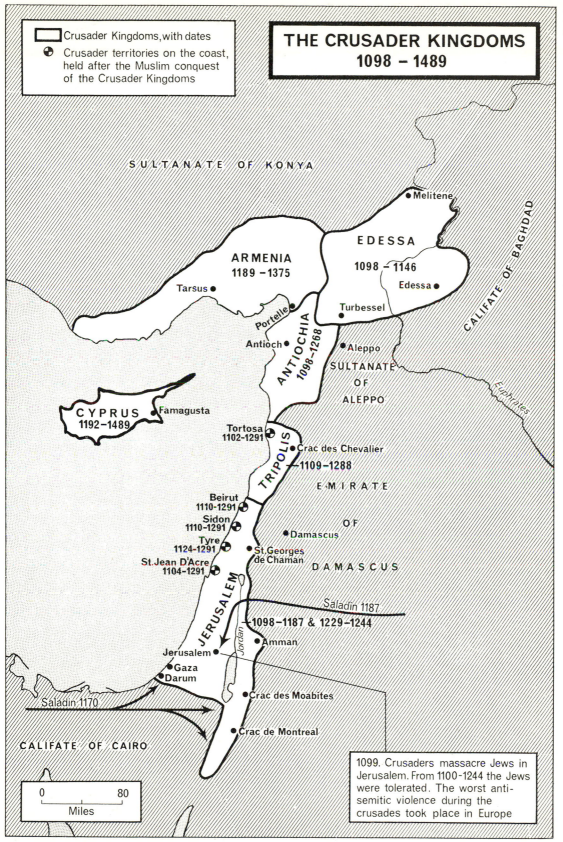

THE CRUSADER KINGDOMS 1098 – 1489

Crusader Kingdoms, with dates

Crusader territories on the coast, held after the Muslim conquest of the Crusader Kingdoms

SULTANATE OF KONYA

CALIFATE OF BAGHDAD

Melitene

EDESSA
1098 – 1146

Edessa

ARMENIA
1189 – 1375

Tarsus

Turbessel

Portelle

Antioch

ANTIOCHIA
1098 – 1268

Aleppo

SULTANATE
OF
ALEPPO

Euphrates

CYPRUS
1192 – 1489

Famagusta

Tortosa
1102 – 1291

Crac des Chevalier
1109 – 1288

TRIPOLIS

E M I R A T E

Beirut
1110 – 1291

Sidon
1110 – 1291

Tyre
1124 – 1291

St Jean D'Acre
1104 – 1291

St Georges
de Chaman

Damascus

O F

D A M A S C U S

JERUSALEM

Saladin 1187

1098 – 1187 & 1229 – 1244

Jordan

Amman

Jerusalem

Gaza

Darum

Crac des Moabites

Saladin 1170

Crac de Montreal

CALIFATE OF CAIRO

0   80
Miles

1099. Crusaders massacre Jews in Jerusalem. From 1100-1244 the Jews were tolerated. The worst anti-semitic violence during the crusades took place in Europe

39

THE JEWS OF ITALY 1000–1600

1584. Each week 150 Jews were compelled to attend conversionist sermons.

"Higgledy piggledy, packed we lie,
Rats in a hamper, swine in a stye,
Wasps in a bottle, frogs in a sieve,
Worms in a carcase, fleas in a sleeve.
Hist! square shoulders, settle your thumbs
And buzz for the bishop – here he comes."
BROWNING, HOLY-CROSS DAY
JEWS AT A CONVERSIONIST SERMON

0 ——— 100
Miles

c.1310. Conference of Italian Jews discussed how to help the persecuted Jews of Germany

1268. Persecution led to total destruction of the Jewish community. Synagogues turned into churches

1550. Jews expelled

1597. 1000 Jews expelled

1000 AD. A Jew was the collector of revenues and director of the mint

1541. The Jews expelled from the Kingdom of Naples. Some settled in northern Italy, others in the Ottoman Empire

887. Jews of Europe first made to wear a "badge of shame" by the Sicilian muslim ruler Ibrahim

Milan · Soncino · Mantua · 1612 · 1516 · Venice · Cremona · 1624 · Pola · Turin · Parma · Ferrara · Genoa · Ravenna · Lucca · Fano · 1571 · Ancona · Pisa · Florence · Livorno · Foligno · Rome 1555 · Gaeta · Lavello · Trani · Bari · Capua · Venosa · Oria · Brindisi · Naples · Matera · Amalfi · Salerno · Taranto · Otranto · KINGDOM OF NAPLES · Messina · Palermo · SICILY · Catania · Syracuse · Gozo · Malta

- ● Jewish communities which existed during the Roman Empire, and were still in existence in 1000 AD
- ◑ Jewish intellectual centres during the Middle Ages
- ◒ Jewish business centres
- ⊙ Other large Jewish communities
- ◉ Ghettoes established under Papal pressure, with dates
- ▦ Area of Papal legislation restricting Jewish rights, 1555. No Jew could own property. All Jews had to wear yellow hats, all Jewesses yellow veils. Conversionist preachers had to be admitted to all synagogues

Massacres of 1391 and 1474, when Sicily was ruled by the House of Aragon. The expulsion of 1492 ended a flourishing community of 40,000 Jews

Jewish communities set up in Roman times. Expelled 1492. From 1539, under Knights of St. John, many Jews were captured in raids on Turkish ships and ports, and formed a "community of slaves" with their own synagogue

THE JEWS OF ENGLAND 1066–1290

- ◉ Towns with Archae, or official registers of Jewish financial transactions
- ● Other towns with Jewish communities, often of only three or four families
- ✪ Towns from which the Jews were expelled before 1290

"All Jews, wherever in the realm they are, must be under the King's protection.... nor can any of them put himself under the protection of any powerful person without the King's licence, because the Jews themselves and all their chattels are the Kings.... If anyone detain them or their money the King may claim them, if he so desire, as his own". **TWELFTH CENTURY LAW**

1190. Violent attack on Jews by crusaders. The Jews killed themselves rather than surrender

1255. Ritual murder charge. 18 Jews executed

1281. Synod forbids Jews to hold public office

Newcastle

Lancaster

York
Beverley
Doncaster
Grimsby
Lincoln

Derby
Nottingham
King's Lynn
Norwich
Stamford
Leicester
Thetford
Bungay
Eye
Coventry
Huntingdon
Bury St. Edmunds
Warwick
Northampton
Cambridge
Worcester
Newport
Bedford
Ipswich
Hereford
Sudbury
Dunstable
Hitchin
Colchester
Gloucester
Oxford
Hertford
Wallingford
Berkhampsted
Cricklade
Wycombe
Marlborough
Reading
London
Bristol
Faversham
Devizes
Newbury
Windsor
Rochester
Wells
Guildford
Canterbury
Wilton
Winchester
Rye
Romsey
Winchelsea
Southampton
Arundel
Dorchester
Chichester
Bosham
Exeter

Beaumaris
Newborough
Flint
Carnarvon
Conway
Rhuddlan
Criccieth
Bala
Harlech

0   50
Miles

The first Jews came to England from Rouen with William the Conqueror. They were mostly moneylenders, dealing both with the King and his barons. After 1189, under the impetus of the crusades, they were much persecuted, fined, assaulted, and expelled from particular towns. In 1290 all 5000 were expelled, and crossed to France and Flanders, having had all their property confiscated.

THE JEWS OF OXFORD 1090–1290

All Saints' Church

St. Martin's Church

LA BOUCHERIE (HIGH STREET)

GREAT BAILEY (QUEEN ST.)

CARFAX

LITTLE JURY LANE

KEPEHARM'S LANE

(Present BLUE BOAR LANE)

SCHITEBARNE LANE

SHIDYERD STREET

ST. EDWARD STREET

Dominican Priory

PENNYFARTHING STREET

1221. Founded so that monks "b[y] their exemplary carriage and gif[t] preaching" might convert the Je[ws] of Oxford to Christianity

St. Aldate's Church

GREAT JEWRY OR FISH STREET (ST. ALDATES)

ST. FRIDESWIDE LANE

Churchyard of St. Frideswide

(Present gatehouse of Christ Church)

SLEYING LANE

St. Michael at the South Gate

Oxford houses known to have been owned by Jews. Many were of stone.

The Synagogue

In 1177 Jews were allowed to buy land outside London. Their first Oxford purchase was land for a cemetery known as "The Jews' Garden"

In 1309, after the expulsion, the synagogue became a tavern, "Broadyates", known by 1520 as the "Dolphin". (Now part of Christ Church)

The Jewish cemetery in use 1231-1290 (now part of the Botanical Gardens)

Part of the Jewish cemetery taken over by the Hospital of St. John. In 1255 Jewish converts to Christianity were living here (Now part of Magdalen College)

East Gate

The Jew, Jacob, sold two of his houses to Walter of Merton, who thus obtained land for Oxford's first residential College. Between 1267 and 1290 Merton bought more Jewish property in both London and Basingstoke

(Magdalen Bridge)

4N'S STREET (MERTON STREET)

River Cherwell

3. After a Jew broke a crucifix, the Jews were ...e to provide a silver crucifix for University ...essions and to erect a stone crucifix in ...quadrangle of Merton College, at that time ...only University quadrangle in existence

1090	First Jewish families settle in Oxford
1141	Jews houses burnt by King Stephen
1210	Much Jewish property confiscated by King John
1220's	Influx of Jews from London, Winchester, Worcester and Lincoln, attracted by business opportunities which were offered by the growing number of University students needing loans
1222	Robert of Reading, a University student, adopts Judaism and marries a Jewess. As a result he was burnt alive
1222	Council of Oxford orders all Jews to wear a yellow star above the left breast on all clothing
1244	Students attack and loot Jewish houses. Jewish loan rate to students fixed by the King at two pence in the pound per week
1255	Influx of Jewish converts to Christianity who received allowance of 1½d a day
1260's	Jews let out rooms to students
1290	Expulsion. All Jewish property granted to the Provost of Wells

FORCIBLE CONVERSIONS 460-1858

1827 Nicholas I of Russia introduced a 25 year military service for Jews, hoping to produce a generation of de-Judaized Jews. Children were recruited at the age of 12, forced to eat pork, cruelly treated and forcibly converted. The law, strengthened in 1850, continued until 1874.

1838 Entire Jewish community forcibly converted to Islam.

460 AD All Jewish children forcibly converted

Widespread forcible conversions

● Forcible conversions with dates

0   300

Miles

Meshed ●

PERSIA

Isfahan ●

CAUCASUS

Volga

Don

UKRAINE
1648 – 1656

Vistula

Cracow
1407

Danube

BYZANTIUM

During the Byzantine Empire there were four major campaigns of forcible conversion in 640, 721, 873 and 930.

Rhine

Worms
1096

Paris
629

Loire

Clermont
576

Limoges
1010

Arles
591

Toulouse
1431

Marseilles
591

Ferrara 1584, 1817

Ancona
1735

Bologna

Rome
1543, 1783

Tunis
1146

Ebro

PORTUGAL
1497

SPAIN
1146, 1391,
1411 and 1492

1858 Papal gendarmes siezed the 6 year old Edgar Mortara, who had been christened by his Catholic nurse while he was ill. Not only Jews throughout Europe, but Napoleon III and the Emperor Franz-Joseph protested. But the boy was brought up a Catholic and filled with a hatred of Judaism. He died in Belgium in 1940.

43

JEWISH GHETTOES 1215-1870

300 Miles

RUSSIA

THE PALE OF SETTLEMENT

Pera (a suburb of Constantinople)

B Y Z A N T I U M

Rhodes 1310-1522

Patras
Modon Coron

Buda 1279

Kazimierz 1494

Posen

Breslau 1266

Prague 1473

Vienna 1570

Venice 1517

Ferrara 1624

Florence 1571

Rome 1215

Naples

1556-1870

Palermo 1312

Frankfurt 1460-1864

Mainz

Verona 1605

Mantua 1612

Turin 1400

Tarascon 1378

Oxford 1222

Barcelona 1350

Valencia 1390

Murcia 1412

Madrid 1480

SPAIN

PORTUGAL

Fez 1450

1662 Jews compelled to move to "swine's dungheap"

Jews lived in parts of towns called the "juderia"

Before 1497 Jews lived in "Judiaria". If found outside the ghetto, during the night they were whipped through the streets

● Principal ghettoes established by order of the city or state authorities, within which the Jews were forced to live

▦ Countries in which the Jews lived in close-knit communities, subject to legal penalties if they moved outside their part of the town

■ The Pale of Settlement within which the majority of Russian Jews were forced to live 1835-1917

▨ Muslim North Africa, where Jews lived in a special quarter, the Mellah, but were not subjected to the same restrictions and indignities as in Christian Europe

★ Church Councils which decreed that Jews must wear a special badge on their clothes. Sometimes this took the form of a yellow Star of David

44

HEBREW PRINTING PRESSES 1441-1860

RUSSIA

Black Sea

OTTOMAN EMPIRE

Aegean Sea

Mediterranean Sea

North Sea

Atlantic Ocean

POLAND

GERMANY
1500-1550

FRANCE

SPAIN

PORTUGAL

Safed
1563

Constantinople
1503

Smyrna
1764

Odessa
1860

Salonica
1500

Reggio
1475

Rome
1486

1475-1550

Venice
1516

Vilna
1860

Grodno
1789

Lemberg
1788

Lyck
1856

Lublin
1571

Cracow
1592

Berlin
1798

Prague
1513

Hamburg
1711

Amsterdam
1627

Antwerp
1523

Strasbourg
1509

Basel
1516

Zurich
1526

Geneva
1556

Paris
1508

Avignon
1444

Soncino
1483

Nice
1773

London
1563

Guadalajara
1482

Lisbon
1489

Faro
1487

Fez
1516

0 miles 300

0 kilometres 400

Important printing presses, publishing Hebrew books, with date of first known publication

Important printings of Jewish prayer books

Areas of widespread Jewish printing presses 1475-1500 and 1500-1550

First weekly newspapers printed in Hebrew

© Martin Gilbert 1985

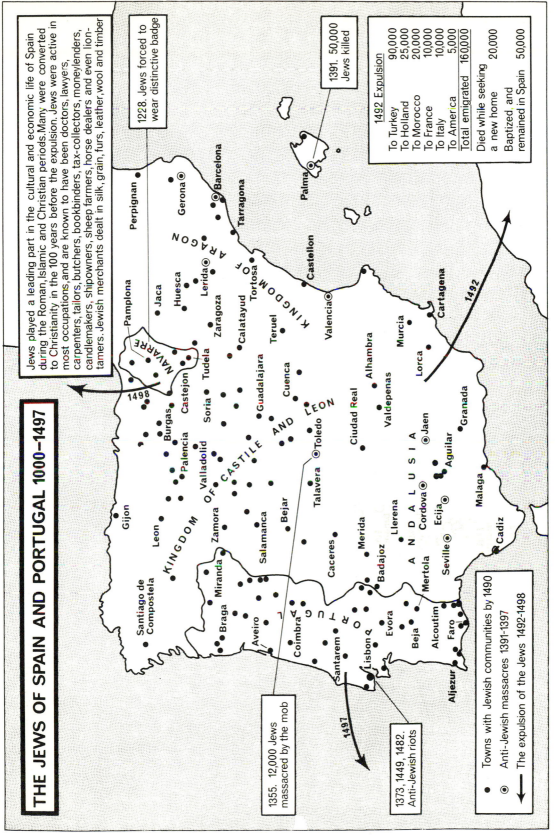

THE JEWS OF SPAIN AND PORTUGAL 1000–1497

Jews played a leading part in the cultural and economic life of Spain during the Roman, Islamic and Christian periods. Many were converted to Christianity in the 100 years before the expulsion. Jews were active in most occupations, and are known to have been doctors, lawyers, carpenters, tailors, butchers, bookbinders, tax-collectors, moneylenders, candlemakers, shipowners, sheep farmers, horse dealers and even lion-tamers. Jewish merchants dealt in silk, grain, furs, leather, wool and timber

1228. Jews forced to wear distinctive badge

1391. 50,000 Jews killed

1492 Expulsion	
To Turkey	90,000
To Holland	25,000
To Morocco	20,000
To France	10,000
To Italy	10,000
To America	5,000
Total emigrated	160,000
Died while seeking a new home	20,000
Baptized and remained in Spain	50,000

1355. 12,000 Jews massacred by the mob

1373, 1449, 1482. Anti-Jewish riots

• Towns with Jewish communities by 1490
◉ Anti-Jewish massacres 1391-1397
→ The expulsion of the Jews 1492-1498

KINGDOM OF ARAGON

KINGDOM OF CASTILE AND LEON

NAVARRE

ANDALUSIA

PORTUGAL

Perpignan
Barcelona
Gerona
Tarragona
Castellon
Palma
Pamplona
Jaca
Huesca
Lerida
Tortosa
Zaragoza
Calatayud
Teruel
Valencia
Cartagena
Castejon
Tudela
Soria
Guadalajara
Cuenca
Murcia
Burgas
Palencia
Valladolid
Ciudad Real
Alhambra
Valdepenas
Lorca
Gijon
Leon
Zamora
Bejar
Talavera
Toledo
Jaen
Granada
Santiago de Compostela
Miranda
Salamanca
Caceres
Merida
Llerena
Cordova
Ecija
Aguilar
Malaga
Braga
Coimbra
Evora
Seville
Cadiz
Aveiro
Santarem
Lisbon
Beja
Alcoutim
Faro
Mertola
Badajoz
Aljezur

1498
1492
1497

46

EXPULSIONS 1000-1500

WALES 1290
1290 ENGLAND
1290
Hamburg
Amsterdam
HOLLAND
FLANDERS Antwerp
Paris 1182
FRANCE
GERMANY
1306
1306
1420
Turin
Udine
1394
1394
Venice
Genoa
PROVENCE
1394
Livorno
1490
ITALY
1497
NAVARRE
1492
Rome
PORTUGAL
SPAIN
1492
Naples
1492
1497
SARDINIA
1492
1492
1492
To
BRAZIL
1492
Algiers
1492
SICILY
Oran
Tunis
Fez
Tlemcen
M   A   G   H   R   E   B
Tripoli

Jewish communities with date of expulsion

Direction of the flight and dispersal of expelled Jews,
mostly to Poland, Italy and the Ottoman Empire

Principal places of resettlement

LITHUANIA

1445
1495
1495
1495

R U S S I A

0   200
Miles

*"O God, thou hast cast us
off, thou hast scattered us,
thou hast been displeased;
O turn thyself to us again."*
PSALM 60

⊙ Grodno
⊙ Bialystok

96-1192
⊙ Posen
Kalisz ⊙ ⊙
⊙ Lodz
Radom
⊙
Brest-
Litovsk
⊙
⊙ Pinsk

⊙ Chernigov
⊙ Kiev
⊙ Kharkov

48
SILESIA
1159
⊙ Lublin
Lutzk ⊙
Cracow
1494
⊙ Lemberg
Zhitomir
⊙
⊙ Tarnopol

48

P O L A N D

1016
1350
1016
1016

TRIA   1421

⊙ Kishinev

1349-1360

1016

HUNGARY

CRIMEA ○ Theodosia
(Kaffa)

1016

⊙ Trebizond

⊙ Nicopolis

⊙ Spalato
Adrianople

⊙ Cattaro

O T T O M A N

⊙ Constantinople

Salonika ⊙

E M P I R E

⊙
CORFU

⊙ Smyrna

⊙ Damascus

⊙ Safed

⊙ Jerusalem

⊙ CRETE

⊙ Alexandria

Cairo ⊙

O T T O M A N   E M P I R E

O T T O

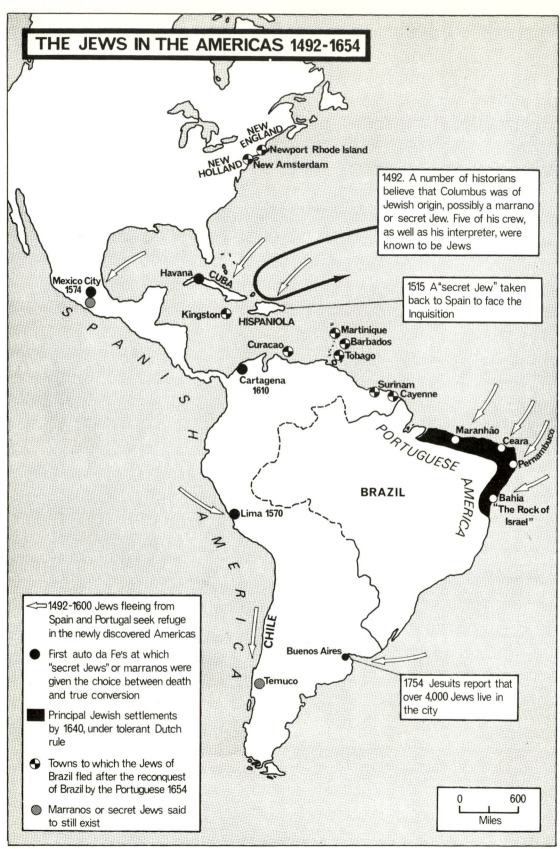

THE JEWS IN THE AMERICAS 1492-1654

NEW ENGLAND

Newport Rhode Island

NEW HOLLAND

New Amsterdam

1492. A number of historians believe that Columbus was of Jewish origin, possibly a marrano or secret Jew. Five of his crew, as well as his interpreter, were known to be Jews

Mexico City 1574

Havana **CUBA**

1515 A "secret Jew" taken back to Spain to face the Inquisition

Kingston

HISPANIOLA

Martinique

Barbados

Curacao

Tobago

Cartagena 1610

Surinam

Cayenne

S P A N I S H

Maranhâo

Ceara

PORTUGUESE

Pernambuco

BRAZIL

AMERICA

Bahia "The Rock of Israel"

Lima 1570

A M E R I C A

CHILE

Buenos Aires

Temuco

1754 Jesuits report that over 4,000 Jews live in the city

1492-1600 Jews fleeing from Spain and Portugal seek refuge in the newly discovered Americas

● First auto da Fe's at which "secret Jews" or marranos were given the choice between death and true conversion

■ Principal Jewish settlements by 1640, under tolerant Dutch rule

◑ Towns to which the Jews of Brazil fled after the reconquest of Brazil by the Portuguese 1654

◐ Marranos or secret Jews said to still exist

0   600
Miles

THE JEWS OF RUSSIA
1545 – 1837

--- Russia in 1650

Annexations of 1654 give Russia its first large Jewish communities. Many of the Jews were at once murdered

Centres of conversion to judaism 1796-1825. In 1825 all settlements were destroyed and the converts banished to Siberia and the Caucasus

Expulsion of the Jews, with dates

1837. Burning and banning of Jewish books

1825. Tsar Alexander sees a Jewish family making tin-plate, an occupation forbidden to Jews . The family were at once deported, and local authorities warned "that the rules concerning the Jews must be observed with all possible stringency"

1563. Jews who refused baptism drowned

1545. Jewish goods from Poland burnt in public, as Jews forbidden to visit or trade in Moscow

St.Petersburg

Luga

1829

Baltic Sea

Western frontier of Russia in 1795

Polotzk
Vitebsk

Moscow

Mstislav

Tula

Moghilev
1827

Starokonstantinov

Saratov
Orlov

Bobrov

Pavlovsk

Kiev 1829

1830

1829 Nikolaev 1829

CRIMEA
1829 Sebastopol

1829

Black Sea

1708. Peter the Great halts pogrom and allows Jews into St.Petersburg

1827. Jewish rebellion against the law which forced certain Jews to do 25 years military service

"It is not convenient to allow Jews to come with their goods into Russia, since many evils result from them. For they import poisonous herbs [= medicines] and lead astray Russians from Christianity"

IVAN IV 1550

1800. Seen by Abraham Peretz, a wealthy Jew of St.Petersburg, as a possible home for the Jews of Russia, where they would escape the harsh Tsarist laws

0   200
Miles

THE SECRET JEWS OF SPAIN AND PORTUGAL 1492-1930

0 100
Miles

"Against truth, force does not prevail"
MARRANO POEM 1665

1492-1600. Some marranos found refuge in Bordeaux and Bayonne

"New Christians" known as Chuetas

- Towns in which marranos faced the Inquisition, and had either to renounce their judaizing, or be burnt at the stake
- Towns where secret Jews openly practised their Judaism by 1930, following the emancipation of Portuguese Jewry in 1910

British from 1704, providing marranos with a way out of Spain. A number went to Britain, others to Holland and Italy

Many of the Jews who chose conversion in 1492 to avoid expulsion continued to practice Judaism in secret. They were known as "conversos", "New Christians" or "marranos". If discovered, they were handed over to the Inquisition

1836. A British traveller meets a secret Jew

1506. Widespread "slaying of New Christians"

1755. Last death by burning of a secret Jew

FRANCE

Pyrenees

S P A I N

PORTUGAL

MAJORCA

Palma

Barcelona

Saragossa

Valencia

Murcia

Logrono

Cuenca

Valladolid

Madrid

Toledo
Talavera

Granada

Cordoba

Seville

Llerena

Gibraltar

Santiago

Braganza
Vila Real
Escalhao
Pinhel
Coimbra
Fundao
Covilhao
Porto

Lisbon

JEWS UNDER TURKISH RULE
1500–1914

10,000 Jews calling themselves Hebraeli. Carpet weavers, vineyard workers, pedlars and gardeners.

The "Mountain Jews." Rug-makers and leather workers. 30,000 in 1900. Their language, Tat, is basically Persian written in Hebrew characters.

85,000 Jews, mostly refugees from Russia, by 1914

0 — 300 Miles

10,000 Karaite Jews See Maps 27 and 88

1769, 1806. Jews suffer greatly in the wars between Turkey and Russia

Ottoman Empire by 1660. Over a million Jews by 1660. Many had fled from Spanish and Cossack persecution.

Ottoman Empire in 1900. 500,000 Jews.

Areas of continuous Jewish settlement 900–1900.

Jewish cave dwellers or troglodytes. Each Jewish village has its own synagogue and rabbi. There are probably more than 10,000 of these Jews living in the desert mountains, many underground or in high rock forts. They have lived here without interruption for 2,000 years.

1500–1800 Haven for Jews fleeing persecution from Spain, Italy, Germany, Ukraine, Poland, Rumania and Russia.

Under Turkish rule 1518-1830. Jews had to wear a black skullcap and grey cloak and hood.

1574 Turks drive out Spaniards and Jewish community of 4000 flourishes as vineyard cultivators and wine merchants.

1551 Turks encourage settlement of Spanish Jews.

1500. Turks encourage Jewish merchants and physicians to settle in Asia Minor.

DAGHESTAN
Baku
Derbent
CAUCASIA
Tiflis
KURDISTAN
HAMADAN
Mosul
MESOPOTAMIA
Baghdad
YEMEN
PALESTINE
CRIMEA
Constantinople
Jassy
Galatz
Bursa
Smyrna
EGYPT
RUMANIA
BULGARIA
Adrianople
Salonika
BOSNIA
DALMATIA
Dubrovnik
CYRENAICA
Benghazi
Tripoli
Djerba Island
TRIPOLITANIA
Tunis
TUNISIA
Algiers
ALGERIA

51

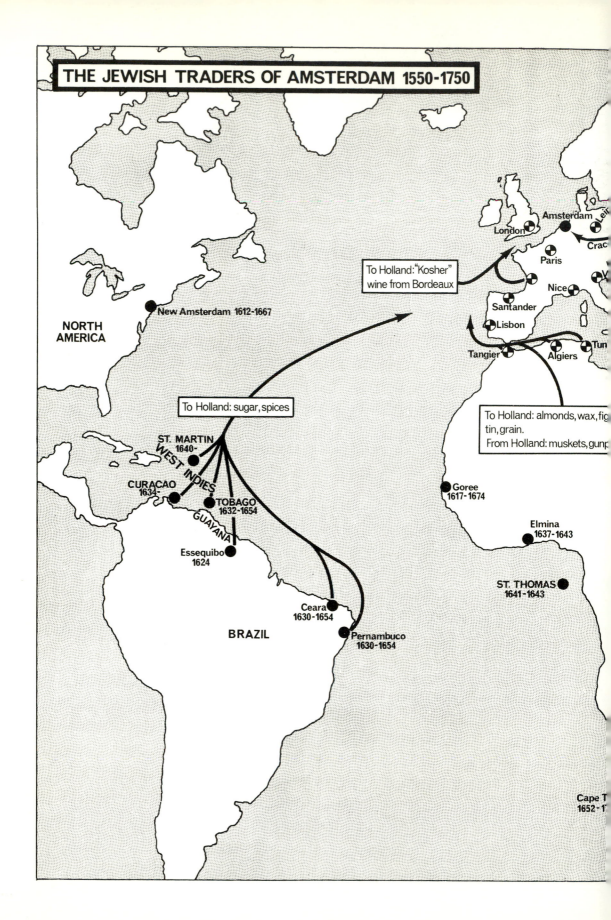

THE JEWISH TRADERS OF AMSTERDAM 1550-1750

Amsterdam
London
Crac
Paris
Nice
Santander
Lisbon
Tangier
Algiers
Tun

To Holland: "Kosher" wine from Bordeaux

New Amsterdam 1612-1667

NORTH AMERICA

To Holland: sugar, spices

To Holland: almonds, wax, fig tin, grain.
From Holland: muskets, gunp

ST. MARTIN 1640-
WEST INDIES
CURACAO 1634-
TOBAGO 1632-1654
GUAYANA

Goree 1617-1674

Essequibo 1624

Elmina 1637-1643

Ceara 1630-1654

BRAZIL

Pernambuco 1630-1654

ST. THOMAS 1641-1643

Cape T
1652-1

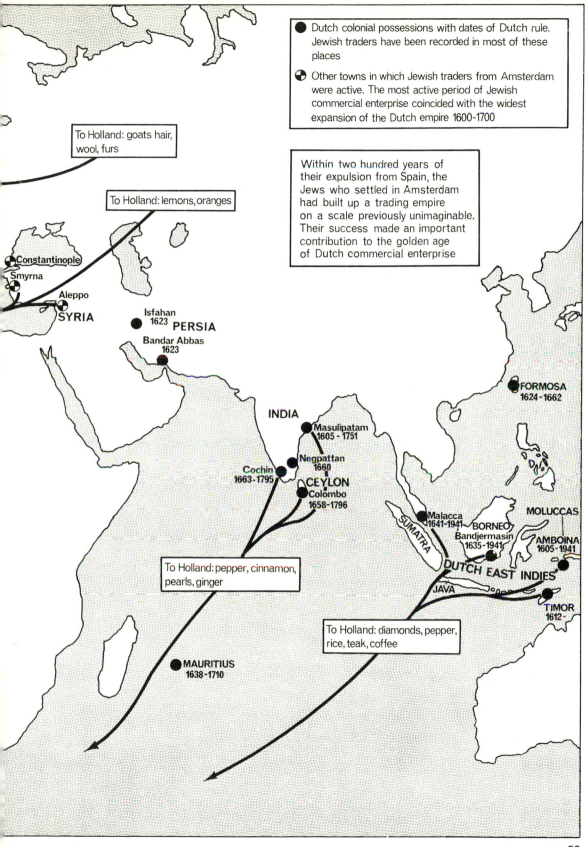

- ● Dutch colonial possessions with dates of Dutch rule. Jewish traders have been recorded in most of these places
- ◑ Other towns in which Jewish traders from Amsterdam were active. The most active period of Jewish commercial enterprise coincided with the widest expansion of the Dutch empire 1600-1700

Within two hundred years of their expulsion from Spain, the Jews who settled in Amsterdam had built up a trading empire on a scale previously unimaginable. Their success made an important contribution to the golden age of Dutch commercial enterprise

To Holland: goats hair, wool, furs

To Holland: lemons, oranges

Constantinople

Smyrna

Aleppo

SYRIA

Isfahan
1623 PERSIA

Bandar Abbas
1623

FORMOSA
1624-1662

INDIA

Masulipatam
1605-1751

Negpattan
1660

Cochin
1663-1795

CEYLON

Colombo
1658-1796

Malacca
1641-1941

SUMATRA

MOLUCCAS

BORNEO
Bandjermasin
1635-1941

AMBOINA
1605-1941

DUTCH EAST INDIES

JAVA

TIMOR
1612

To Holland: pepper, cinnamon, pearls, ginger

To Holland: diamonds, pepper, rice, teak, coffee

MAURITIUS
1638-1710

FALSE MESSIAHS 400-1816

In times of persecution, uncertainty or extreme poverty, many Jews turned for relief to "false" messiahs, many of whom offered to bring them back to Jerusalem. In many cases few details survive about these men; in some cases even their names are unknown

0 ___ 300
Miles

750 Obayah Abu-Iss of Isfahan

800 called Judah Judghan

c.1100 called Chadd

720 called Serene

1147 David Alroy Waged war against the Persians. Intended to lead an army to Jerusalem

c.1000 called Menahem

Tigris

Euphrates

1730 Jacob Querido

1648-1676 Sabbatai Zevi

Smyrna

c. 400 Tried to lead the Jews dry-shod to Jerusalem

1726 Yankiev Leibowitz Frank. Agitation by his followers continued until 1816

Salonica

1700 Michael Cardoso

CRETE

1720 Mordecai Mokiah

Solomon Molcho. Burnt at Mantua by the Inquisition in 1530

Lemberg

Eisenstadt

1720-1726 Nehemiah Hiyya-Hayyun

Prague

Danube

Rhine

1502 Asher Lämmlein

Venice

Padua

1284 Abraham Abulafia

SICILY

Amsterdam

1740 Moses Hayyim Luzzatto

1087

1290 Samuel

1290 Abraham

Ayllon

Cisneros

Avila

Cordova

1117

1127

Fez

1393 Moses Botarel

1522 David Reubeni

PORTUGAL

"Thou, O God, hast promised to redeem us: hasten therefore the period of our redemption... The enemy wounds our heart, throws stones at us, afflicts us, treads us underfoot, and scoffs both at us and our hope for redemption... But the daughter of Zion may indeed rejoice for our Messiah cometh"

JEWISH PRAYER

53

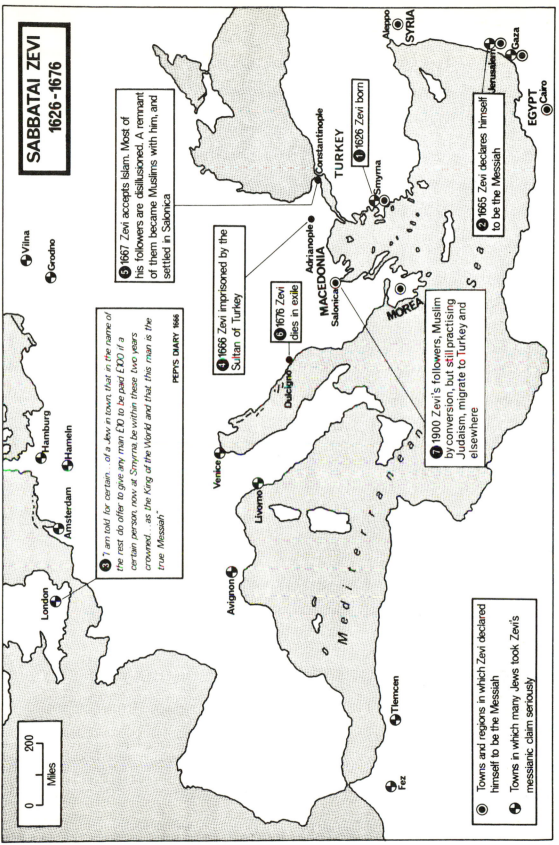

SABBATAI ZEVI
1626-1676

1 1626 Zevi born

2 1665 Zevi declares himself to be the Messiah

3 "I am told for certain...of a Jew in town that in the name of the rest do offer to give any man £10 to be paid £100 if a certain person, now at Smyrna, be within these two years crowned...as the King of the World and that this man is the true Messiah"

PEPY'S **DIARY** 1666

4 1666 Zevi imprisoned by the Sultan of Turkey

5 1667 Zevi accepts Islam. Most of his followers are disillusioned. A remnant of them became Muslims with him, and settled in Salonica

6 1676 Zevi dies in exile

7 1900 Zevi's followers, Muslim by conversion, but still practising Judaism, migrate to Turkey and elsewhere

Vilna

Grodno

Hamburg

Hameln

Amsterdam

London

Avignon

Venice

Livorno

Fez

Tlemcen

Constantinople

TURKEY

Smyrna

Adrianople

MACEDONIA

Salonica

MOREA

Dulcigno

Aleppo

SYRIA

Jerusalem

Gaza

EGYPT

Cairo

Mediterranean Sea

Sea

● Towns and regions in which Zevi declared himself to be the Messiah

◓ Towns in which many Jews took Zevi's messianic claim seriously

0   200
Miles

54

COURT JEWS 1500-1800

Leffman Behrends 1630-1714.
Secured a rabbinate and special
privileges for Hanover Jews

◉Hanover

◉Brunswick

Israel Jacobson 1768-1828. An
educationalist who established
school for Jews and Christians.
He obtained abolition of poll
tax on Jews in 1815

Samson Wertheimer 1648-1724.
Court banker of Vienna 1690.
Chief Rabbi of Hungary 1719.
Prevented the publication of
anti-semitic books. Established
a fund to assist Palestine paupers
(lasted to 1940)

S A

HESSE

△●Frankfort

Darmstadt△   △Aschaffenburg

△Wertheim

Worms◉

Heidelberg◉

ANSBACH

WÜRTTEMBURG

Joseph Oppenheimer(Jüd Süss)
1698-1738. Finance minister. He
was accused of stealing state
funds. He refused to accept
Christianity and was hanged

FRANCE

Samuel Oppenheimer 1630-1703.
Helped finance Austrian wars
against Turkey and Spain.
Supported those Jews seeking
to settle in Palestine

▨ States with Court Jews in high official regard

● Towns with prominent Court Jews

△ Towns where, the Court Jew, Wolf Breidenbach
    obtained the abolition of Jewish tolls

◉ Leading Court Jews

Berlin

Dresden

P O L A N D

Hereditary rights bestowed on Jacob Bassevi by the Emperor Ferdinand II: "To engage in any business whatever, in any part of the Empire, whether cities, towns or market places, in Prague and Vienna, and other places where Jews are allowed to reside or are not. To acquire property and to reside anywhere he pleases. His property in any form to be free from taxes, imposts and duties. To reside in the Imperial quarters. To be responsible to no tribunal, except the marshal of the court".

Prague

Jacob Bassevi 1580-1634. Loaned money for the thrifty. Gave charity to the poor of Palestine

H A B S B U R G   L A N D S

Vienna

Yossl Rosheim 1480-1554. Brilliant imperial financier. He often interceded on behalf of Jewish communities throughout Europe.

H U N G A R Y

Court Jews, also known as court factors, court agents and hofjuden, were mostly wealthy men who became court favourites, often controlling the financial affairs of their state. The jealousies they aroused often led to the persecution of the whole Jewish community. But many used their influence to win privileges for the Jews in their state

GÖRZ

Trieste

0   50
Miles

THE CHMIELNICKI MASSACRES 1648-1656

● Towns where anti-Jewish massacres took place

Principal Blood Libel accusations east of the River Vistula

6 **Dunajgorod**

7 **Zaslav**

In 1648 the Cossack leader, Bogdan Chmielnicki, led a Cossack revolt against the Polish gentry. After defeating the Polish army, his followers joined with the Polish peasants in attacking the Jews. Spasmodic violence continued for eight years. Over 100,000 Jews were killed; many more were tortured or ill-treated; others fled to Holland, Germany, Bohemia and the Balkans.

Baltic Sea

PRUSSIA

Posen (Poznan)

Piotrkow

Pinczow

Gora Kalwarija

Warsaw

River Vistula

River Vistula

Miedzyrzec

Lublin

Wlodawa

Bug River

Krasnik

Zamosc

Bilgoraj

Tomaszow

Przemysl

Lemberg

Drohobycz

Brest-Litovsk

Kobrin

Vladimir

Kovel

Lutzke

Olyka

Berestechko

Brody

Busk

Zlochev

Zbaraz

Satanov

Kamenetz-Podolsk

Rozyszcze

Pinsk

Ladyzhin

Kolki

Tuchin

Klevan

Rovno

Dubno

Ostrog

Starokonstantinov

Medzhibozh

Bar

Sharograd

Mohilev

Yampol

Byeltzy

Dniester

Vilna

Kovno

Grodno

12

Grodno

LITHUANIA

Minsk

Berezino

Stary Bykhov

Pripet

Mozyr

Ryechitza

Bragin

Loyev

Shepetovka

Zhitomir

Miropol

Chudnov

Ulanov

Letichev

Vinnitsa

Nemirov

Bratzlav

Tulchin

Bershad

Fastov

Makhnovka

Pogrebishche

Kiev

Dnieper

Byelaya

Tzerkov

Pereyaslav

Kanev

Chigirin

Korsun

Borispol

Priluki

Lubny

Konotop

Verkhovka

Chernigov

Oster

Yampol

Borisovka

WHITE RUSSIA

Druya

Polotzk

Nevel

Vitebsk

Dubrovna

Orsha

Kopys

Mstislavl

Krasny

Krichev

Propolsk

Serpeisk

Roslavl

Starodub

Homel

U K R A I N E

0   100

Miles

ANTI-JEWISH 'BLOOD LIBELS', 1407 – 1816

The information on the large map was provided by Mikhail Salman of Leningrad, as a result of his researches.

Throughout the Middle Ages, and beyond, Jews were accused at Easter/Passover time of using the blood of murdered Christian children in the baking of Passover bread. This map shows twenty of these 'blood libel' ritual murder accusations in the Vistula region, several of the executions that followed, as well as the acquittals of 1815 and 1816.

© Martin Gilbert 1985

Poznan
1736-40

Gostynin
1576

River Vistula

River Vistula

Warsaw

River Bug

Sochaczew
1556 **3** *executed*
1619 *executions*

Leczyca
1639 **2** *executed*

Siedlce
1617 *executions*
1816 *acquitted*

Bielsk
1564
1 *executed*

Wlodawa
1816 *acquitted*

Miedzyrzec
1815 *acquitted*

Lublin
1598 **1** *executed*
1636 **2** *executed*
1713
1816 *acquitted*

Sandomierz
1605 *executions*
1690 **1** *executed*
1710

Vistula

River Vistula

Cracow
1407
1637

Olkusz
1 *executed*

BLOOD LIBELS 1144 - 1407

This map shows towns in which, between 1144 and 1407, Jews were falsely accused of killing Christians in order to use their blood for so-called 'ritual purposes'.

Bug

Warsaw

Vistula

0 miles 200

Lincoln
Norwich
London
Winchester

Paris
Seine

Blois

Boppard
Metz
Endingen
Rhine

Fulda

Pforzheim
Munich

Prague

Velhartice

Constance
Berne

Rhône

Valréas

Saragossa

0   miles   50
0 kilometres 80

NAPOLEON AND THE JEWS

0   300
Miles

1800-1815. British subsidies to her European allies in the war against Napoleon handled by the Rothschilds

1805. Napoleon forms a Jewish battalion, which fights at Waterloo

1807. Napoleon convenes Grand Sanhedrin of 45 rabbis and 25 lay Jews, which declares that Jews are not a national but a purely religious community

1806. Napoleon curtails Jewish moneylending

1812. Jews support Russians as they fear Napoleon's liberalism as a threat to their orthodoxy

1813. Jews distinguish themselves in the Prussian Army against Napoleon

"Bonaparte a fait publier une proclamation, dans laquelle il invite tous les juifs de l'Asie et de l'Afrique à venir se ranger sous ses drapeaux pour rétablir l'ancienne Jérusalem"

REPORT IN THE MONITEUR 1799

1799. Jews join Turks in preparing to defend the city against Napoleon

"Ce n'est pas seulement pour rendre aux juifs leur Jérusalem que Bonaparte a conquis la Syrie: il avait de plus vastes dessins....de marcher sur Constantinople, pour jeter de là l'épouvante dans Vienne et Petersbourg."

THE MONITEUR 1799

WHITE RUSSIA

R U S S I A

PRUSSIA

WESTPHALIA

AUSTRIA

Constantinople

Leipzig

Frankfurt 1811

Venice 1797

Rome 1810

Mainz 1798

ALSACE

BATAVIA

Waterloo

Paris

St.Jean D'Acre

Jérusalem

Cairo

Alexandria

- ● Ghettoes which Napoleon freed, with dates
  These ghettoes were all restored after Napoleon's fall in 1815

- → Napoleon's march on Constantinople, checked by the British in 1799

- ▨ Jews of Westphalia fully emancipated in 1807 by Napoleon's brother, Jerome

- ▨ Jews of Hamburg, Mecklenburg, Lübeck and Bremen granted full civil rights by France in 1811

THE EMANCIPATION OF EUROPEAN JEWRY 1789–1918

"And if, in the course of many centuries, the oppressed descendants of warriors and sages have degenerated from the qualities of their fathers; if while excluded from the blessings of law, and bowed down under the yoke of slavery, they have contracted some of the vices of outlaws and slaves, shall we consider this as a matter of reproach to them? Shall we not rather consider it as a matter of shame and remorse to ourselves? Let us open to them every career in which ability and energy can be displayed. Till we have done this, let us not presume to say that there is no genius among the countrymen of Isaiah, no heroism among the descendants of the Maccabees."
MACAULAY IN 1833

GREAT BRITAIN
1858 Jews could be elected to Parliament
1871 Jews could enter University
1890 Full emancipation

Emancipation gave the Jews full civil equality

Bordeaux 1790

SPAIN

Only European country not granting civil equality to Jews by 1919

→ PORTUGAL 1910

NORWAY 1851
SWEDEN 1865
DENMARK 1848
HOLLAND 1796
BELGIUM 1830
PRUSSIA 1850
BRUNSWICK 1834
SAXONY 1868
GERMANY 1871
HESSE CASSEL 1833
Frankfurt 1811
Mainz 1798
BADEN 1862
SWITZERLAND 1874
ALSACE 1791
Avignon 1790
PIEDMONT 1848
Venice 1797
ITALY 1848–1870
Rome 1810 ROME 1870

RUSSIA 1917
RUMANIA 1918
SERBIA
BULGARIA
AUSTRIA-HUNGARY 1867
THE OTTOMAN EMPIRE 1908

Emancipation imposed by Bismarck and Disraeli at Berlin Congress 1878

Frontiers of 1900

⊕ Ghettoes freed by Napoleon, but subsequently restored

0   200
Miles

THE ROTHSCHILD FAMILY 1760-1914

Legend

- ◣ First Rothschild bank, about 1760
- ◢ Banking Houses with dates of foundation set up by the sons of Mayer Rothschild
- ⊘ Major loans to finance Government expenditure for wars, industry etc.
- ◖ Important investments by Rothschild banks
- ✕ Loan refused on account of Russia's anti-semitic policies
- ※ Rival Catholic bank established, but collapsed Rival London bank, Barings, collapsed, but was then sustained by Rothschilds 1893 Portuguese Government accepts loan from rival Jewish bankers, Sterns
- ▨ Major philanthropic activity of members of the Rothschild family

St. Petersburg

Loan to Britain for Irish famine

Invalids Kitchen 1859
Home For Aged Incurables 1859

PRUSSIA
● Berlin
1815

HANOVER

FRANKFURT

Wittkowitz Iron Works

Hospital 1869
Orphan Asylum
Home for Poor Musicians

● 1816
▲ Vienna

Idra silver mines

※ 1805 ● London

Paris ● 1817 ✂

1866 Primary School
1874 Orphanages
1904 Poorhouses

FRANCE

HESSE
● BADEN
BAVARIA

Dalmatian asphalt lake

LUCCA

PAPAL
STATES

Naples
1821

Rio Tinto copper mines

SPAIN

Almaden mercury mines

PORTUGAL

◎ BRAZIL

GREECE

TURKEY ⊘

Baku Oil Fields ◣

Loan to Britain and France for Crimean War against Russia
1854

Agricultural Colonies bought for Zionist settlers 1887

Loan to Britain for Suez Canal shares 1876

During the Civil War in the United States, 1861-1865, the Rothschilds lost money heavily by their support for the bonds of the southern Confederate States, who were defeated in 1865

0   300
Miles

60

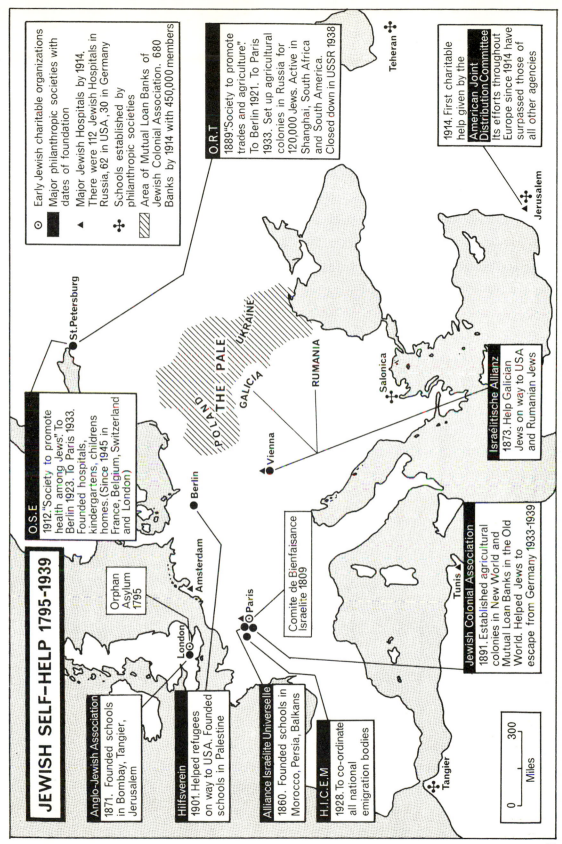

JEWISH SELF-HELP 1795-1939

Legend:

- ⊙ Early Jewish charitable organizations
- ■ Major philanthropic societies with dates of foundation
- ▲ Major Jewish Hospitals by 1914. There were 112 Jewish Hospitals in Russia, 62 in USA, 30 in Germany
- ✣ Schools established by philanthropic societies
- ▨ Area of Mutual Loan Banks of Jewish Colonial Association. 680 Banks by 1914 with 450,000 members

O.R.T
1889."Society to promote trades and agriculture". To Berlin 1921. To Paris 1933. Set up agricultural colonies in Russia for 120,000 Jews. Active in Shanghai, South Africa and South America. Closed down in USSR 1938

1914. First charitable help given by the **American Joint Distribution Committee** Its efforts throughout Europe since 1914 have surpassed those of all other agencies

O.S.E
1912."Society to promote health among Jews". To Berlin 1923. To Paris 1933. Founded hospitals, kindergartens, childrens homes. (Since 1945 in France, Belgium, Switzerland and London)

Orphan Asylum 1795

Anglo-Jewish Association
1871. Founded schools in Bombay, Tangier, Jerusalem

Hilfsverein
1901. Helped refugees on way to USA. Founded schools in Palestine

Alliance Israélite Universelle
1860. Founded schools in Morocco, Persia, Balkans

H.I.C.E.M
1928. To co-ordinate all national emigration bodies

Comite de Bienfaisance Israelite 1809

Israélitische Allianz
1873. Help Galician Jews on way to USA and Rumanian Jews

Jewish Colonial Association
1891. Established agricultural colonies in New World and Mutual Loan Banks in the Old World. Helped Jews to escape from Germany 1933-1939

Map labels: St.Petersburg, POLAND, THE PALE, UKRAINE, GALICIA, RUMANIA, Salonica, Vienna, Berlin, Amsterdam, London, Paris, Tunis, Tangier, Teheran, Jerusalem

0 300
Miles

THE JEWS OF NORTH AMERICA 1654-1860

100 / 0
Miles

Quebec

Three Rivers

Montreal **1768**

St. Lawrence

5 1758 Abraham Gradis stores goods for the French army in the war against Britain

8 1780 Abraham Hart establishes a trading post for Indians

C A N A D A

L. Ontario

L. Erie

Cleveland **1839**

6 1770 Levi Solomon founds a trading post

Mackinac

L. Huron

L. Superior

L. Michigan

Green Bay

9 1794 Jacob Franks opens trading post with Indians

Chicago **1837**

Vincennes

Cincinnati **1824**

17 1854 Rabbi Isaac Wise sets up first Reform congregation

Louisville **1832**

15 1850's Adam Gimbel, an itinerant peddlar, lays the foundation of a department store empire

St. Louis **1839**

Boston **1652**

Newport, Rhode Island

New Amsterdam (New York)

Newark **1852**

Wawarsing

Philadelphia **1747**

Easton

Lancaster

Baltimore **1842**

Richmond **1789**

Chryslers Farm

1 1654 First Jewish community of 23 Dutch Jews, fleeing from the introduction of the Inquisition in Pernambuco

2 1680 Jews from Surinam and Curacao form second community

13 1824-1852 Influx of German Jews. Synagogue building was bought from the Coloured Presbyterian Church in New York

14 1837 Jewish agricultural colony, established by German Jews, fails after ten years

3 1728 Jews allowed to build their first synagogue

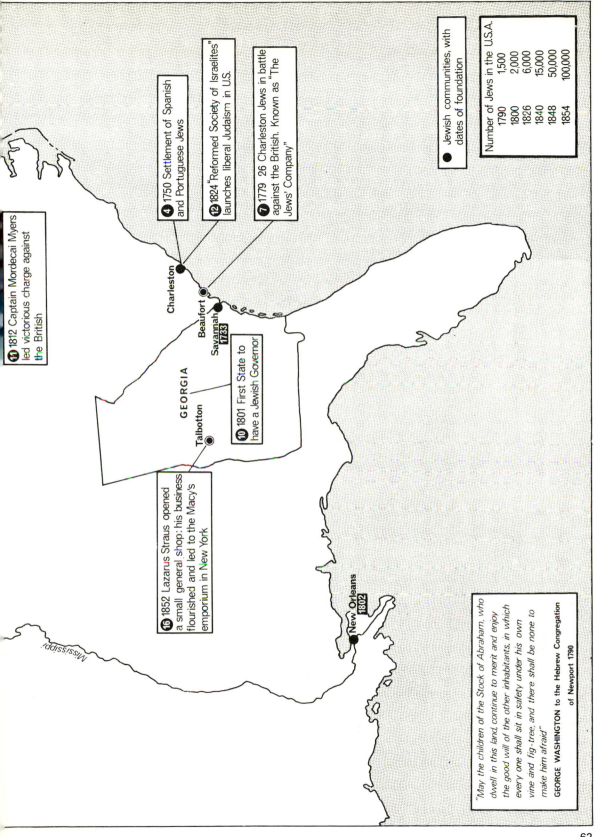

11 1812 Captain Mordecai Myers led victorious charge against the British

4 1750 Settlement of Spanish and Portuguese Jews

12 1824 "Reformed Society of Israelites" launches liberal Judaism in U.S.

7 1779 26 Charleston Jews in battle against the British. Known as "The Jews' Company"

Charleston
Beaufort
Savannah **1733**

GEORGIA

Talbotton

10 1801 First State to have a Jewish Governor

16 1852 Lazarus Straus opened a small general shop: his business flourished and led to the Macy's emporium in New York

Mississippi

New Orleans **1802**

● Jewish communities, with dates of foundation

Number of Jews in the U.S.A.	
1790	1,500
1800	2,000
1826	6,000
1840	15,000
1848	50,000
1854	100,000

"May the children of the Stock of Abraham, who dwell in this land, continue to merit and enjoy the good will of the other inhabitants, in which every one shall sit in safety under his own vine and fig-tree, and there shall be none to make him afraid"

GEORGE WASHINGTON to the Hebrew Congregation of Newport 1790

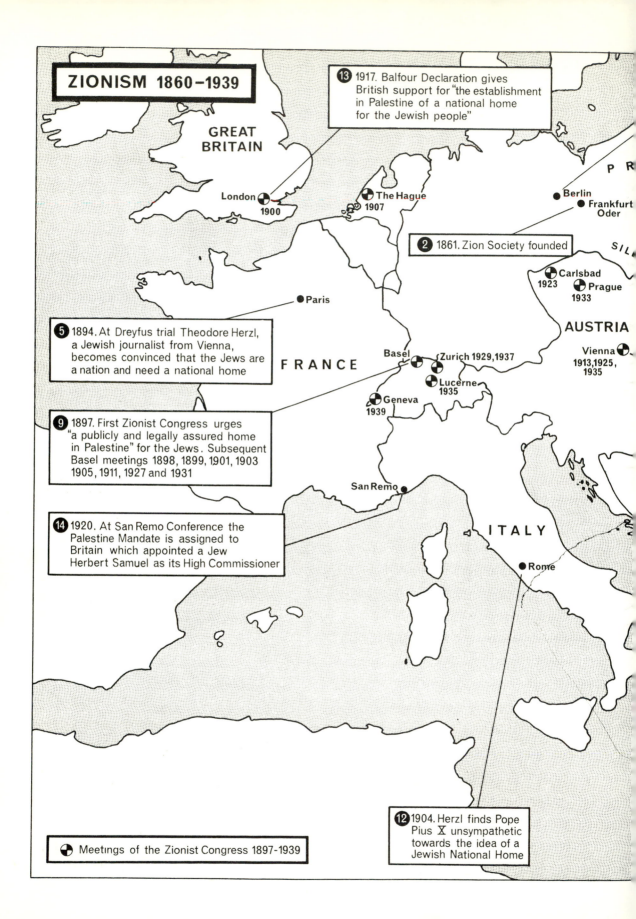

ZIONISM 1860–1939

GREAT BRITAIN

13 1917. Balfour Declaration gives British support for "the establishment in Palestine of a national home for the Jewish people"

London 1900

The Hague 1907

Berlin

Frankfurt Oder

PR...

2 1861. Zion Society founded

SIL...

Carlsbad 1923

Prague 1933

Paris

AUSTRIA

Vienna 1913,1925, 1935

5 1894. At Dreyfus trial Theodore Herzl, a Jewish journalist from Vienna, becomes convinced that the Jews are a nation and need a national home

FRANCE

Basel

Zurich 1929,1937

Lucerne 1935

Geneva 1939

9 1897. First Zionist Congress urges "a publicly and legally assured home in Palestine" for the Jews. Subsequent Basel meetings 1898, 1899, 1901, 1903 1905, 1911, 1927 and 1931

San Remo

ITALY

14 1920. At San Remo Conference the Palestine Mandate is assigned to Britain which appointed a Jew Herbert Samuel as its High Commissioner

Rome

12 1904. Herzl finds Pope Pius X unsympathetic towards the idea of a Jewish National Home

⬕ Meetings of the Zionist Congress 1897–1939

3 1882. Leo Pinsker in "Auto-Emancipation" urged Jews to seek a national retreat, preferably on the banks of the Jordan

● Vilna

S S I A

● Thorn

11 1903. Herzl acclaimed "Herzl the King" during visit to Russia

1 1860. Conference discusses possibility of a Jewish home in Palestine

● Kattowitz

R U S S I A

HUNGARY

4 1884. "Lovers of Zion" movement holds conference

Odessa ●

6 1896. Herzl publishes his "Jews' State" urging the Jews to seek their national home in Palestine. Its immediate impact was on Russian Jewry

8 1897. "Lovers of Zion" revitalized by Herzl, and by its new President, Ussishkin, a disciple of Ahad Ha-am, the spiritual prophet of Zionism

B U L G A R I A

Constantinople ●

7 1896. Herzl acclaimed as the Messiah

T U R K E Y

10 1901 Herzl has audience with Sultan. Asks in vain for Palestine as a Jewish national home

0   200
Miles

EUROPEAN ANTI-SEMITISM 1845-1914

0   200
Miles

1903. First publication of "Protocols of Zion" claiming to reveal a Jewish world conspiracy

1866-1914. Government support of anti-semitism led to the flight of 70,000 of Rumania's 125,000 Jews, mostly to the United States

RUSSIA

Saratov 1853

Kutais 1878

CRIMEA

Kiev 1913

UKRAINE

BESSARABIA

St. Petersburg

LITHUANIA

WHITE RUSSIA

POLAND

GALICIA

RUMANIA

BULGARIA

1892. Synagogue burnt by the mob

Neu-Stettin

1879 Anti-semitism supported by many intellectuals

1881 Anti-Semitic League active

1882 Anti-Semitic Party wins Parliamentary seats

AUSTRIA   1882

Tizsa-Eszlar

Vienna 1897-1910 Anti-semitic Mayor speaks and legislates against Jews

HUNGARY

Linz Anti-semitic Party launched 1885

1884-1904. Frequent mob violence against Jews

GERMANY

Xanten 1882

ITALY

1911. Anti-Jewish riots by Welsh miners. Jewish shops looted

GREAT BRITAIN

Tredegar

FRANCE

Anti-semitic books published by Toussenel (1845), Gobineau (1854) and Drumont (1886).

1894-1906. Strong anti-semitic feeling aroused when Dreyfus, a French Jewish Officer, was accused of selling military secrets to Germany

⊕ Ritual Murder charges. These often led to mob violence against the Jews, who were accused of using the blood of Christian children to mix with their Passover bread

▨ Anti-Jewish violence organised by the "Union of the Russian People", or "Black Hundreds" founded in 1905. Two million Jews fled from Russia, mostly to the United States

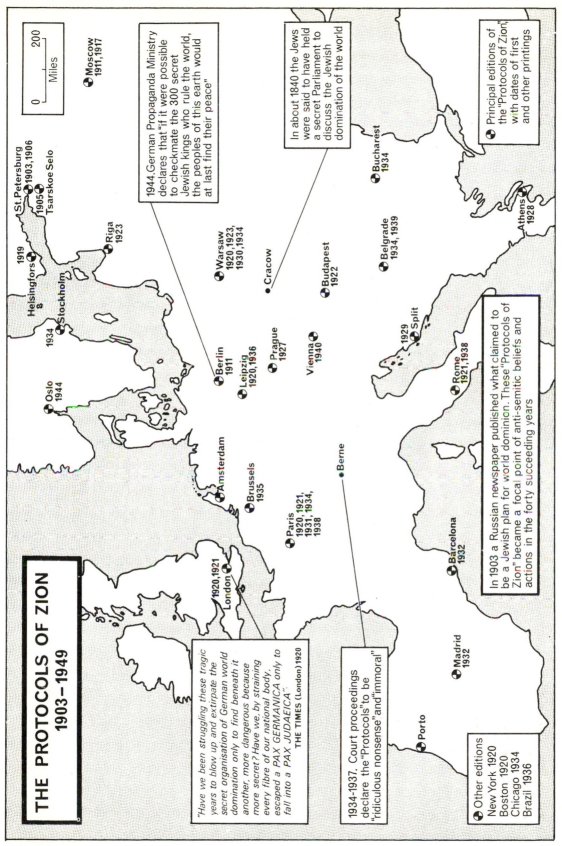

THE PROTOCOLS OF ZION
1903–1949

"Have we been struggling these tragic years to blow up and extirpate the secret organisation of German world domination only to find beneath it another, more dangerous because more secret? Have we, by straining every fibre of our national body, escaped a PAX GERMANICA only to fall into a PAX JUDAEICA".
THE TIMES (London) 1920

1934–1937. Court proceedings declare the "Protocols" to be "ridiculous nonsense" and "immoral"

Other editions
New York 1920
Boston 1920
Chicago 1934
Brazil 1936

In 1903 a Russian newspaper published what claimed to be a Jewish plan for world dominion. These "Protocols of Zion" became a focal point of anti-semitic beliefs and actions in the forty succeeding years

1944.German Propaganda Ministry declares that "if it were possible to checkmate the 300 secret Jewish kings who rule the world, the peoples of this earth would at last find their peace"

In about 1840 the Jews were said to have held a secret Parliament to discuss the Jewish domination of the world

Principal editions of the "Protocols of Zion", with dates of first and other printings

Moscow
1911, 1917

St.Petersburg
1903, 1906
1905
Tsarskoe Selo

Riga
1923

Helsingfors
1919

Stockholm
1934

Warsaw
1920, 1923,
1930, 1934

Cracow

Budapest
1922

Bucharest
1934

Belgrade
1934, 1939

Athens
1928

Berlin
1911

Leipzig
1920, 1936

Prague
1927

Vienna
1940

Split
1929

Oslo
1944

Rome
1921, 1938

Amsterdam

Brussels
1935

Berne

Barcelona
1932

Paris
1920, 1921,
1931, 1934,
1938

London
1920, 1921

Madrid
1932

Porto

0   200
Miles

THE LEGEND OF THE WANDERING JEW

According to legend, while Christ was carrying his cross to Calvary he paused, hoping to rest on a Jew's doorstep. The man at once drove him away, crying out, "Go hence! Go hence!" Christ then replied: "I go, but ye will roam the earth until I come again."

The "Wandering Jew" was reported in upper New York State in 1898. In 1940 an insurance agent believing himself to be the "Wandering Jew" studied biographies of himself at the New York Public Library and had visiting card printed T.W. Jew

Verily I say unto you, there be some standing here, which shall not taste of death till they see the Son of Man coming in his kingdom."

MATTHEW 16,28

ESTONIA
LITHUANIA
Mansurian Lakes
SWEDEN
Lübeck 1603
Hamburg 1542
Hanover
Breslau 1646
SILESIA
Leipzig 1642
Bamberg
Prague 1602
Munich 1721
CARINTHIA
Villach
TYROL
UKRAINE

Jutland
Schleswig
Jade Bay
Amsterdam
1700 Paderborn
Brussels 1640
WURTTEMBURG
Basel
Grimsel
Zermatt
Cambridge 1710
Ypres 1623
Paris 1604
Hull 1769
London 1818
CARMARTHEN
GLAMORGAN
BRITTANY

Avignon 1784
Florence 1320,1411
Siena
SICILY

Toledo 1547

Lesbos
Dembre
Attalia
Syme
Janina

THE LEGEND OF THE WANDERING JEW

0   300
Miles

Areas and towns which the "Wandering Jew" was said to have visited in the Middle Ages

Towns in which men claimed to be the "Wandering Jew" with dates

66

JEWISH CABINET MINISTERS AND COMMISSARS 1848-1948

Jewish Cabinet Ministers in parliamentary democracies, with the **year** of the entry of the first Jew to the Cabinet.

Leading Jewish Communist Ministers, with the **year** of the first to enter office.

Frontiers of 1919-1937

400

Miles

0

SOVIET RUSSIA
1917

RUMANIA
1947

FINLAND

ESTONIA

LATVIA

LITH-
UANIA

POLAND
1947

BULGARIA

GREECE

T U R K E Y

CZECHOSLOVAKIA
1948

1919
HUNGARY

1919

YUGOSLAVIA
1945

ALBANIA

NORWAY

SWEDEN

DENMARK
1911

GERMANY
1918

BAVARIA

1919

AUSTRIA

SWITZ.

1870

I T A L Y

HOLLAND
1860

BELGIUM

FRANCE
1848

1909

UNITED
KINGDOM

EIRE

S P A I N

PORTUGAL

67

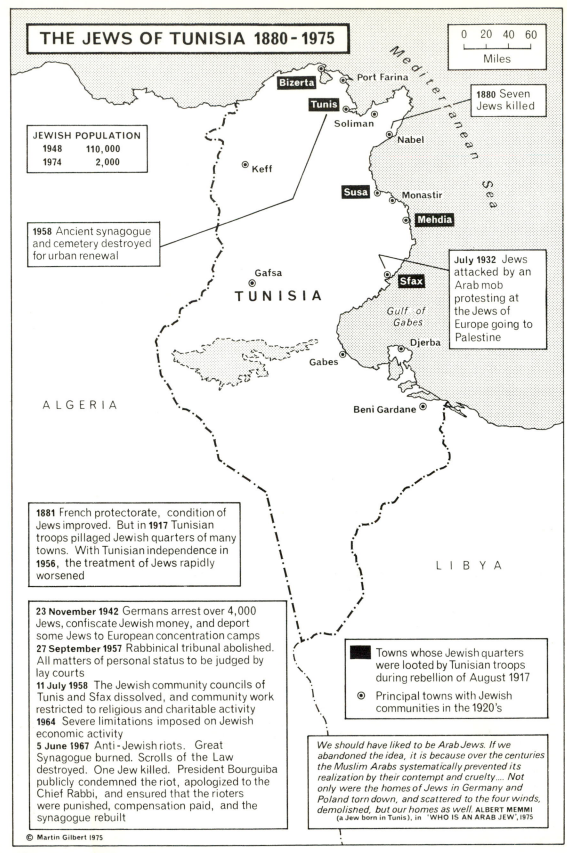

THE JEWS OF TUNISIA 1880-1975

0 20 40 60
Miles

Mediterranean Sea

Bizerta

Port Farina

Tunis

Soliman

1880 Seven Jews killed

Nabel

JEWISH POPULATION
1948   110,000
1974   2,000

Keff

Susa

Monastir

Mehdia

1958 Ancient synagogue and cemetery destroyed for urban renewal

July 1932 Jews attacked by an Arab mob protesting at the Jews of Europe going to Palestine

Gafsa

TUNISIA

Sfax

Gulf of Gabes

Djerba

Gabes

ALGERIA

Beni Gardane

LIBYA

1881 French protectorate, condition of Jews improved. But in **1917** Tunisian troops pillaged Jewish quarters of many towns. With Tunisian independence in **1956**, the treatment of Jews rapidly worsened

23 November 1942 Germans arrest over 4,000 Jews, confiscate Jewish money, and deport some Jews to European concentration camps
27 September 1957 Rabbinical tribunal abolished. All matters of personal status to be judged by lay courts
11 July 1958 The Jewish community councils of Tunis and Sfax dissolved, and community work restricted to religious and charitable activity
1964 Severe limitations imposed on Jewish economic activity
5 June 1967 Anti-Jewish riots. Great Synagogue burned. Scrolls of the Law destroyed. One Jew killed. President Bourguiba publicly condemned the riot, apologized to the Chief Rabbi, and ensured that the rioters were punished, compensation paid, and the synagogue rebuilt

Towns whose Jewish quarters were looted by Tunisian troops during rebellion of August 1917

Principal towns with Jewish communities in the 1920's

We should have liked to be Arab Jews. If we abandoned the idea, it is because over the centuries the Muslim Arabs systematically prevented its realization by their contempt and cruelty.... Not only were the homes of Jews in Germany and Poland torn down, and scattered to the four winds, demolished, but our homes as well. ALBERT MEMMI (a Jew born in Tunis), in 'WHO IS AN ARAB JEW', 1975

© Martin Gilbert 1975

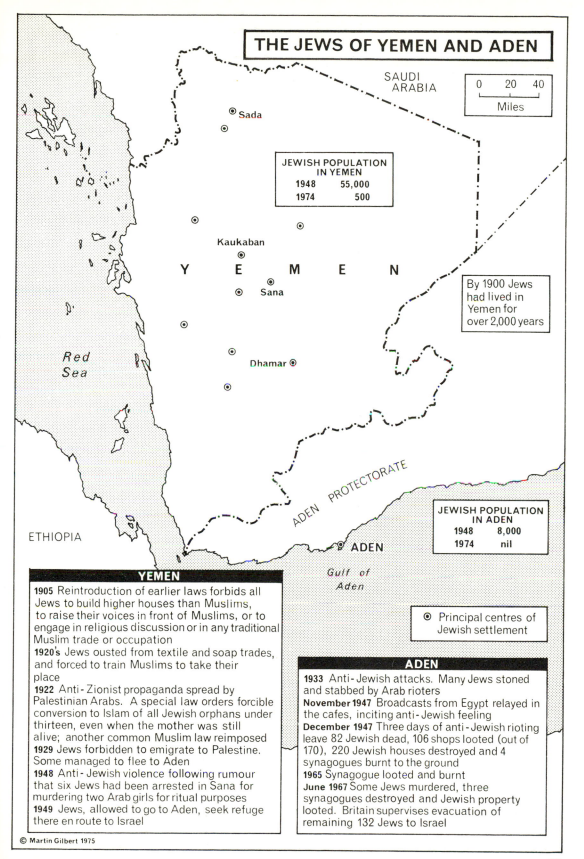

THE JEWS OF YEMEN AND ADEN

SAUDI
ARABIA

0	20	40
Miles

⦿ Sada

**JEWISH POPULATION
IN YEMEN**
1948   55,000
1974   500

Y   E   M   E   N

Kaukaban
⦿

⦿ Sana

By 1900 Jews
had lived in
Yemen for
over 2,000 years

*Red
Sea*

Dhamar ⦿

ADEN PROTECTORATE

ETHIOPIA

⦿ ADEN

**JEWISH POPULATION
IN ADEN**
1948   8,000
1974   nil

*Gulf of
Aden*

⦿ Principal centres of
Jewish settlement

YEMEN

1905 Reintroduction of earlier laws forbids all
Jews to build higher houses than Muslims,
to raise their voices in front of Muslims, or to
engage in religious discussion or in any traditional
Muslim trade or occupation
1920's Jews ousted from textile and soap trades,
and forced to train Muslims to take their
place
1922 Anti-Zionist propaganda spread by
Palestinian Arabs. A special law orders forcible
conversion to Islam of all Jewish orphans under
thirteen, even when the mother was still
alive; another common Muslim law reimposed
1929 Jews forbidden to emigrate to Palestine.
Some managed to flee to Aden
1948 Anti-Jewish violence following rumour
that six Jews had been arrested in Sana for
murdering two Arab girls for ritual purposes
1949 Jews, allowed to go to Aden, seek refuge
there en route to Israel

© Martin Gilbert 1975

ADEN

1933 Anti-Jewish attacks. Many Jews stoned
and stabbed by Arab rioters
November 1947 Broadcasts from Egypt relayed in
the cafes, inciting anti-Jewish feeling
December 1947 Three days of anti-Jewish rioting
leave 82 Jewish dead, 106 shops looted (out of
170), 220 Jewish houses destroyed and 4
synagogues burnt to the ground
1965 Synagogue looted and burnt
June 1967 Some Jews murdered, three
synagogues destroyed and Jewish property
looted. Britain supervises evacuation of
remaining 132 Jews to Israel

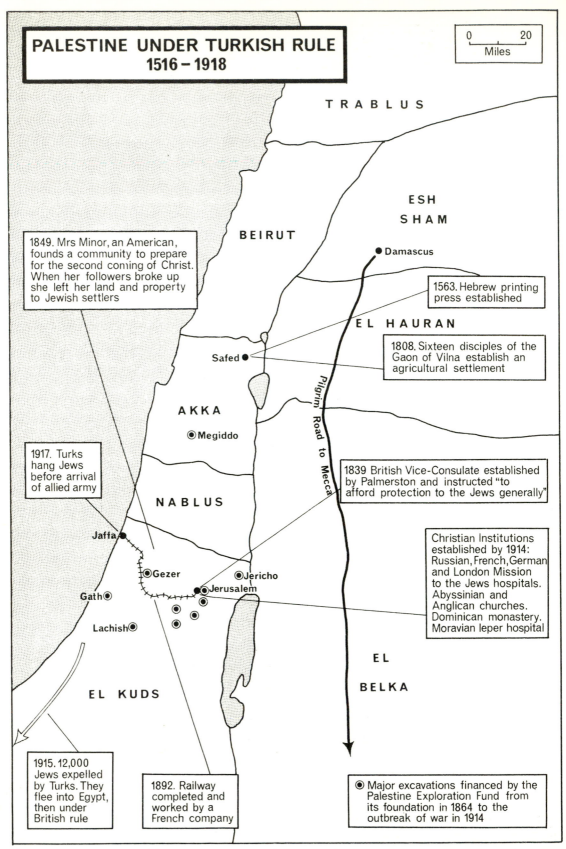

PALESTINE UNDER TURKISH RULE
1516 – 1918

0   20
Miles

T R A B L U S

E S H

S H A M

● Damascus

B E I R U T

1849. Mrs Minor, an American, founds a community to prepare for the second coming of Christ. When her followers broke up she left her land and property to Jewish settlers

1563. Hebrew printing press established

E L   H A U R A N

1808. Sixteen disciples of the Gaon of Vilna establish an agricultural settlement

Safed ●

Pilgrim Road to Mecca

A K K A

⊙ Megiddo

1917. Turks hang Jews before arrival of allied army

1839 British Vice-Consulate established by Palmerston and instructed "to afford protection to the Jews generally"

N A B L U S

Christian Institutions established by 1914: Russian, French, German and London Mission to the Jews hospitals. Abyssinian and Anglican churches. Dominican monastery. Moravian leper hospital

Jaffa ●

⊙ Gezer

Gath ●

⊙ Jericho

● Jerusalem

Lachish ●

E L   K U D S

E L

B E L K A

1915. 12,000 Jews expelled by Turks. They flee into Egypt, then under British rule

1892. Railway completed and worked by a French company

⊙ Major excavations financed by the Palestine Exploration Fund from its foundation in 1864 to the outbreak of war in 1914

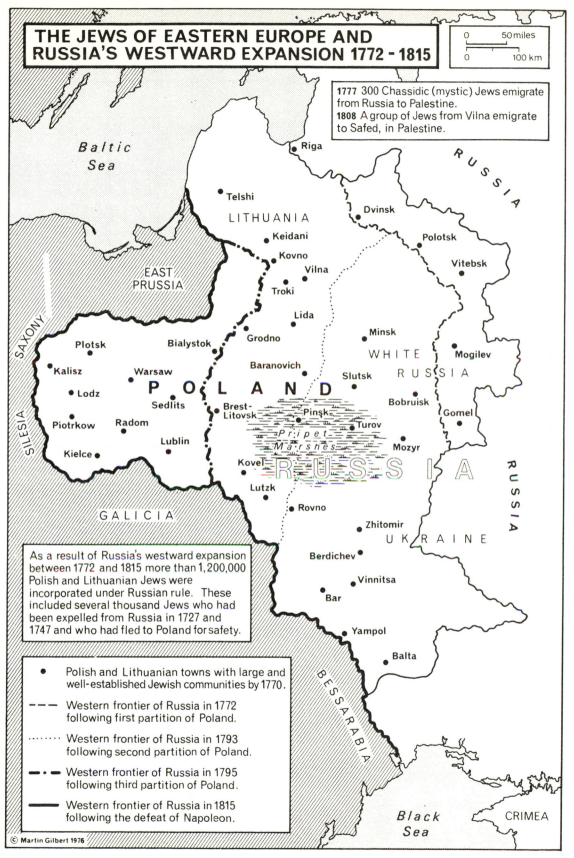

THE JEWS OF EASTERN EUROPE AND RUSSIA'S WESTWARD EXPANSION 1772 - 1815

0   50 miles
0   100 km

1777 300 Chassidic (mystic) Jews emigrate from Russia to Palestine.
1808 A group of Jews from Vilna emigrate to Safed, in Palestine.

Baltic Sea

RUSSIA

• Riga

• Telshi

LITHUANIA

• Dvinsk

• Keidani

• Polotsk

• Kovno

EAST PRUSSIA

• Vilna

• Vitebsk

• Troki

• Lida

SAXONY

• Minsk

• Plotsk

• Bialystok

• Grodno

WHITE RUSSIA

• Mogilev

• Kalisz

• Warsaw

• Baranovich

• Slutsk

P O L A N D

• Lodz

• Sedlits

• Brest-Litovsk

• Pinsk

• Bobruisk

• Gomel

SILESIA

• Piotrkow

• Radom

Pripet Marshes

• Turov

• Lublin

• Mozyr

• Kielce

• Kovel

R U S S I A

• Lutzk

GALICIA

• Rovno

• Zhitomir

U K R A I N E

As a result of Russia's westward expansion between 1772 and 1815 more than 1,200,000 Polish and Lithuanian Jews were incorporated under Russian rule. These included several thousand Jews who had been expelled from Russia in 1727 and 1747 and who had fled to Poland for safety.

• Berdichev

• Vinnitsa

• Bar

• Yampol

RUSSIA

• Balta

BESSARABIA

•   Polish and Lithuanian towns with large and well-established Jewish communities by 1770.

– – – Western frontier of Russia in 1772 following first partition of Poland.

········· Western frontier of Russia in 1793 following second partition of Poland.

–·–·– Western frontier of Russia in 1795 following third partition of Poland.

——— Western frontier of Russia in 1815 following the defeat of Napoleon.

© Martin Gilbert 1976

Black Sea

CRIMEA

THE JEWISH PALE OF SETTLEMENT IN RUSSIA, 1835 - 1917

In 1882 500,000 Jews living in rural areas of the Pale were forced to leave their homes and live in towns or townlets (shtetls) in the Pale. 250,000 Jews living along the western frontier of Russia were also moved into the Pale. 700,000 Jews living east of the Pale were driven into the Pale by 1891.

1891 2,000 Jews deported many of them in chains.

1891 20,000 Jews expelled.

SWEDEN

Baltic Sea

GERMANY

Lake Pskov

St. Petersburg
21,000

Novgorod
4,700

Lake Ilmen

BALTIC PROVINCES
80,000

KOVNO

VITEBSK

SUWALKI

VILNA

Moscow
9,000

Smolensk
10,500

MOGILEV

Tula
2,700

PLOCK

LOMZA

GRODNO

KALISZ

WARSAW

SEDLITS

MINSK

Pripet Marshes

R U S S I A

PIOTRKOW

RADOM

LUBLIN

KIELCE

VOLHYNIA

CHERNIGOV

Kursk
4,000

Voronezh
2,700

AUSTRIA-HUNGARY

Kiev

KIEV

POLTAVA

Kharkov
14,000

PODOLIA

By 1897 there were 5 million Jews living in the Pale, and 320,000 outside it, of whom 100,000 lived in Siberia, 80,000 in Baltic Provinces, 50,000 in the Caucasus, 10,000 in Russian Central Asia and 10,000 in Astrakhan and the Terek region.

RUMANIA

BESSARABIA

KHERSON

Nikolaev

EKATERINOSLAV

T A U R I D A

Sea of Azov

KUBAN
5,000

Sebastopol

Yalta

Black Sea

☐ The Pale of Settlement. Russian Jews were confined to this area by laws of 1795 and 1835. By 1897 there were more than 5 million Jews in the Pale.

⊙ Towns within the Pale which were themselves barred to Jews without special residence permits.

• Towns outside the Pale with Jewish inhabitants (figures for 1897).

0   100m
0   100km

TURKEY

© Martin Gilbert 1976

POVERTY AND CHARITY AMONG RUSSIAN JEWS IN 1900

Provinces of the Pale in which 22% of all Jews were in receipt of poor relief from the Jewish community.

20% on receipt of poor relief, No province in the Pale had less than 14% of its Jews on relief.

O.R.T.

1889 'Society to promote trades and agriculture'. Set up agricultural colonies in Russia for 120,000 Jews. Moved to Berlin 1921, to Paris 1933. Active in Shanghai, South Africa and South Africa.

O.S.E.

1921 'Society to promote health among Jews'. Founded hospitals, kindergartens, children's homes. Moved to Berlin 1923, to Paris 1933. Since 1945 active in France, Belgium, Switzerland and London.

SWEDEN

ESTONIA

Lake Pskov

St.Petersburg

LATVIA

Baltic Sea

Riga

Dvinsk

LITHUANIA

Kovno

GERMANY

Vilna

Minsk

WHITE RUSSIA

Warsaw

THE JEWISH

POLAND

Pripet Marshes

PALE OF SETTLEMENT

R U S S I A

Vladimir Volynsk

AUSTRIA - HUNGARY

Zhitomir

Kremenchug

Berdychev

Poltava

Khotin

Elizavetgrad

Ekaterinoslav

U K R A I N E

RUMANIA

Nikolaev

Odessa

Kherson

CRIMEA

Black Sea

Despite the poverty and pressures of life in the Pale, the years 1835 to 1914 saw a great flourishing of Jewish literary, cultural, political, educational, journalistic, religious and spiritual activity.

Among the charitable societies organised by the Jews were those to supply poor students with clothes, soldiers with kosher food, the poor with free medical treatment, poor brides with dowries and orphans with technical education.

● Cities in which over one in every four of all Jews received free fuel from the Fuel Charities organised by the Jewish community.

⊙ Principal houses of shelter for poor vagrants

At the cheap eating house in Odessa 400 dinners were provided daily, over 150 without charge.

0   50   100 miles
0   150 km

© Martin Gilbert 1976

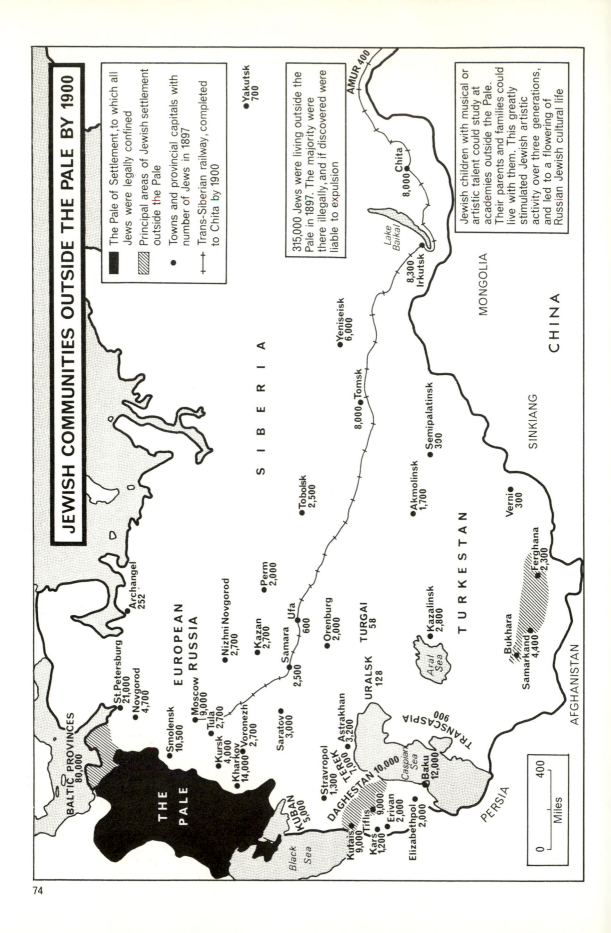

JEWISH COMMUNITIES OUTSIDE THE PALE BY 1900

The Pale of Settlement, to which all Jews were legally confined

Principal areas of Jewish settlement outside the Pale

● Towns and provincial capitals with number of Jews in 1897

+—+ Trans-Siberian railway, completed to Chita by 1900

315,000 Jews were living outside the Pale in 1897. The majority were there illegally, and if discovered were liable to expulsion

Jewish children with musical or artistic talent could study at academies outside the Pale. Their parents and families could live with them. This greatly stimulated Jewish artistic activity over three generations, and led to a flowering of Russian Jewish cultural life

● Yakutsk 700

AMUR 400

● Chita 8,000

MONGOLIA

CHINA

SINKIANG

Lake Baikal

Irkutsk 8,300

● Yeniseisk 6,000

S I B E R I A

8,000 Tomsk

● Tobolsk 2,500

● Semipalatinsk 300

● Akmolinsk 1,700

T U R K E S T A N

● Verni 300

● Ferghana 2,300

● Perm 2,000

Kazan 2,700

Ufa 600

Samara 2,500

Orenburg 2,000

TURGAI 58

Kazalinsk 2,800

Aral Sea

Bukhara

Samarkand 4,400

AFGHANISTAN

EUROPEAN RUSSIA

● Archangel 252

● Nizhni Novgorod 2,700

● St.Petersburg 21,000

Novgorod 4,700

● Smolensk 10,500

● Moscow 19,000

Tula 2,700

Kursk 4,000

Voronezh 2,700

Kharkov 14,000

Saratov 3,000

URALSK 128

Astrakhan 3,200

TRANSCASPIA 900

BALTIC PROVINCES 80,000

THE PALE

KUBAN 5,000

Stavropol 1,300

TEREK 7,000

DAGHESTAN 10,000

Tiflis 9,000

Kutais 9,000

Kars 1,200

Elizabethpol 2,000

Erivan 2,000

Baku 12,000

Caspian Sea

Black Sea

PERSIA

0   400
Miles

74

POGROMS 1871–1906

The word "pogrom" is Russian for "violent mass attack", against a section of the community

"Russia and England are of yesterday, as compared with the imperishable people, which, with an inextinguishable life and immutable traditions, and faith in God and in the laws of God, scattered, as it is, all over the world, passed through the fires unscathed, trampled into the dust and yet never combining with the dust into which it is trampled, lives still, a witness and a warning to us all."
CARDINAL MANNING PROTESTING AGAINST RUSSIAN POGROMS IN 1882

1871. First anti-Jewish pogrom. Jews beaten in the streets. Jewish shops looted and property destroyed

Vologda 1906
Simbirsk 1906
Nizhni Novgorod 1880
Murom 1906
Tsaritsyn 1906
Dusyata 1905
Minsk 1905
Moghilev 1904
Starodub 1891
Rostov-on-Don 1883
Bialystok 1902, 1906
Syedlitz 1905
Brest–Litovsk 1906
Gomel 1903, 1906
Konotop
Nyezhin
Ekaterinoslav 1883
Lodz 1905
Czestochowa 1902
Zhitomir 1905
Kiev
Pereyaslav
Smyela
Elizavetgrad
Melitopol 1905
Simferopol 1905
Balta 1882
Ananayev
Kishinev 1903
Nikolaevka
Odessa

0   100
Miles

The Pale, home of over 4 million Jews

Pogroms of 1881. These attacks on Jews and Jewish property were thought to have been officially instigated

Pogroms 1882–1899. Often caused by peasant economic discontent finding an outlet in anti-Jewish violence

Pogroms 1902–1906. Stimulated by a growing hatred of Jews and encouraged by the Government

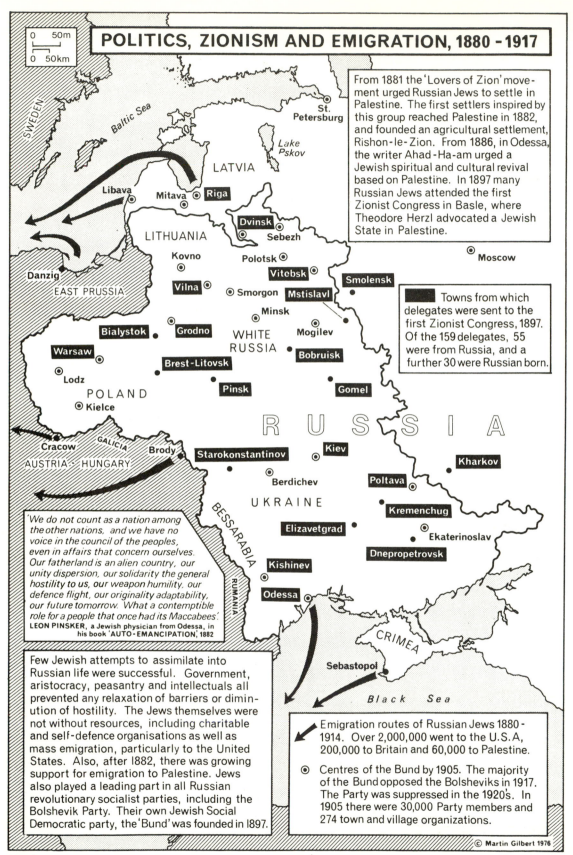

POLITICS, ZIONISM AND EMIGRATION, 1880 - 1917

0 ___ 50m
0 ___ 50km

From 1881 the 'Lovers of Zion' move-ment urged Russian Jews to settle in Palestine. The first settlers inspired by this group reached Palestine in 1882, and founded an agricultural settlement, Rishon-le-Zion. From 1886, in Odessa, the writer Ahad-Ha-am urged a Jewish spiritual and cultural revival based on Palestine. In 1897 many Russian Jews attended the first Zionist Congress in Basle, where Theodore Herzl advocated a Jewish State in Palestine.

SWEDEN

Baltic Sea

St. Petersburg

Lake Pskov

LATVIA

Libava
Mitava ⊙ Riga

LITHUANIA

Dvinsk ⊙
Sebezh

Danzig

EAST PRUSSIA

Kovno ⊙

Polotsk ⊙

Vilna ⊙ Smorgon

Vitebsk ⊙

Smolensk

Mstislavl

Moscow ⊙

Towns from which delegates were sent to the first Zionist Congress, 1897. Of the 159 delegates, 55 were from Russia, and a further 30 were Russian born.

Minsk ⊙

Mogilev

WHITE RUSSIA

Bobruisk

Bialystok

Grodno

Warsaw

Brest-Litovsk

Pinsk

Gomel

Lodz

POLAND

Kielce ⊙

R U S S I A

Cracow

GALICIA

Brody

AUSTRIA - HUNGARY

Starokonstantinov

Kiev ⊙

Kharkov

Berdichev

Poltava ⊙

UKRAINE

Kremenchug

BESSARABIA

Elizavetgrad

Ekaterinoslav

'We do not count as a nation among the other nations, and we have no voice in the council of the peoples, even in affairs that concern ourselves. Our fatherland is an alien country, our unity dispersion, our solidarity the general hostility to us, our weapon humility, our defence flight, our originality adaptability, our future tomorrow. What a contemptible role for a people that once had its Maccabees.'
LEON PINSKER, a Jewish physician from Odessa, in his book 'AUTO-EMANCIPATION', 1882

Dnepropetrovsk

Kishinev

RUMANIA

Odessa

CRIMEA

Sebastopol

Black Sea

Few Jewish attempts to assimilate into Russian life were successful. Government, aristocracy, peasantry and intellectuals all prevented any relaxation of barriers or dimin-ution of hostility. The Jews themselves were not without resources, including charitable and self-defence organisations as well as mass emigration, particularly to the United States. Also, after 1882, there was growing support for emigration to Palestine. Jews also played a leading part in all Russian revolutionary socialist parties, including the Bolshevik Party. Their own Jewish Social Democratic party, the 'Bund' was founded in 1897.

Emigration routes of Russian Jews 1880-1914. Over 2,000,000 went to the U.S.A, 200,000 to Britain and 60,000 to Palestine.

⊙ Centres of the Bund by 1905. The majority of the Bund opposed the Bolsheviks in 1917. The Party was suppressed in the 1920's. In 1905 there were 30,000 Party members and 274 town and village organizations.

© Martin Gilbert 1976

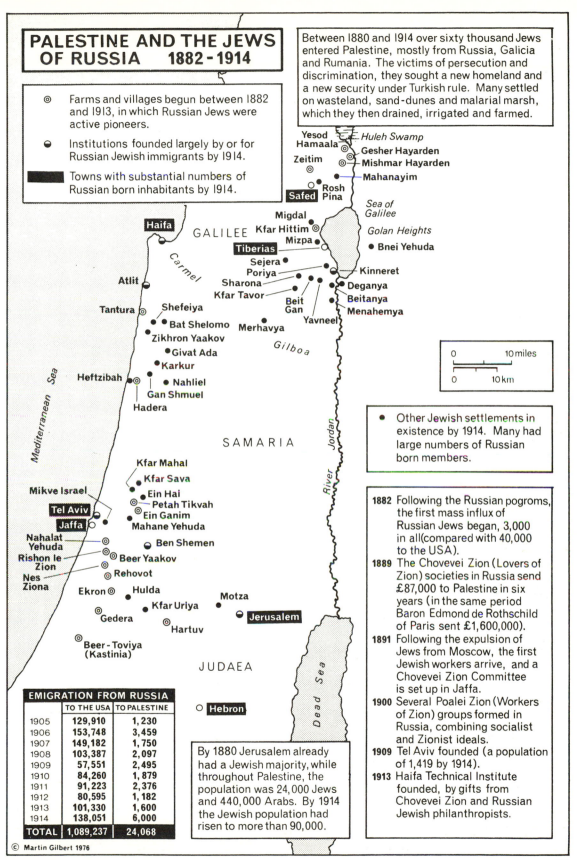

PALESTINE AND THE JEWS OF RUSSIA 1882-1914

Between 1880 and 1914 over sixty thousand Jews entered Palestine, mostly from Russia, Galicia and Rumania. The victims of persecution and discrimination, they sought a new homeland and a new security under Turkish rule. Many settled on wasteland, sand-dunes and malarial marsh, which they then drained, irrigated and farmed.

◉ Farms and villages begun between 1882 and 1913, in which Russian Jews were active pioneers.

◓ Institutions founded largely by or for Russian Jewish immigrants by 1914.

▬ Towns with substantial numbers of Russian born inhabitants by 1914.

Yesod Hamaala
Huleh Swamp
Zeitim
Gesher Hayarden
Mishmar Hayarden
Mahanayim
Rosh Pina
Safed
Sea of Galilee
Migdal
Kfar Hittim
Haifa
GALILEE
Mizpa
Golan Heights
Bnei Yehuda
Tiberias
Sejera
Poriya
Kinneret
Sharona
Deganya
Kfar Tavor
Beitanya
Beit Gan
Menahemya
Yavneel
Atlit
Carmel
Shefeiya
Bat Shelomo
Merhavya
Zikhron Yaakov
Tantura
Gilboa
Givat Ada
Karkur
Heftzibah
Nahliel
Gan Shmuel
Hadera

Mediterranean Sea

SAMARIA

| 0 | 10 miles |
| 0 | 10 km |

● Other Jewish settlements in existence by 1914. Many had large numbers of Russian born members.

Kfar Mahal
Kfar Sava
Mikve Israel
Ein Hai
Petah Tikvah
Tel Aviv
Ein Ganim
Jaffa
Mahane Yehuda
Nahalat Yehuda
Ben Shemen
Rishon le Zion
Beer Yaakov
Nes Ziona
Rehovot
Ekron
Hulda
Motza
Kfar Urlya
Gedera
Jerusalem
Hartuv
Beer - Toviya (Kastinia)

River Jordan

JUDAEA

Dead Sea

○ **Hebron**

1882 Following the Russian pogroms, the first mass influx of Russian Jews began, 3,000 in all (compared with 40,000 to the USA).

1889 The Chovevei Zion (Lovers of Zion) societies in Russia send £87,000 to Palestine in six years (in the same period Baron Edmond de Rothschild of Paris sent £1,600,000).

1891 Following the expulsion of Jews from Moscow, the first Jewish workers arrive, and a Chovevei Zion Committee is set up in Jaffa.

1900 Several Poalei Zion (Workers of Zion) groups formed in Russia, combining socialist and Zionist ideals.

1909 Tel Aviv founded (a population of 1,419 by 1914).

1913 Haifa Technical Institute founded, by gifts from Chovevei Zion and Russian Jewish philanthropists.

EMIGRATION FROM RUSSIA		
	TO THE USA	TO PALESTINE
1905	129,910	1,230
1906	153,748	3,459
1907	149,182	1,750
1908	103,387	2,097
1909	57,551	2,495
1910	84,260	1,879
1911	91,223	2,376
1912	80,595	1,182
1913	101,330	1,600
1914	138,051	6,000
TOTAL	**1,089,237**	**24,068**

By 1880 Jerusalem already had a Jewish majority, while throughout Palestine, the population was 24,000 Jews and 440,000 Arabs. By 1914 the Jewish population had risen to more than 90,000.

© Martin Gilbert 1976

JEWISH MILITARY ACTIVITY 1794–1967

1794. A Jewish Legion of 500 joins the Poles in revolt against Russia

1830. A Jewish Regiment of 800 joins the Poles in revolt against Russia

1941-1944 Jewish partisan groups fight behind the German lines

1881. Jews force would-be pogrom organizers to leave town

1918. Jewish Self-Defence forces are organised in the Ukraine and Galicia against Russian anti-semitic outrages

1917. Jewish Regiment of 5,000 men active in allied conquest of Palestine from the Turks. 1918. 6,000 U.S. Jews join the Regiment

1948,1956,1967. The State of Israel resists and defeats its Arab neighbours

1815. An all-Jewish unit, raised by Napoleon in Batavia in 1805, fights against the British and Prussians. 235 Jews killed at Waterloo

1943. Warsaw Ghetto rising. Principal Jewish revolt against Nazi rule

1944. Palestinian Jewess Hannah Senesch, a student, parachuted into German-occupied Hungary. Captured by Germans and shot

1920. Joseph Trumpeldor killed defending colony against marauding arabs

1944. Enzo Sereni parachuted behind German lines. Caught and killed

1915. Zion Mule Corps founded. Its 500 members fought against the Turks at Gallipoli

"The Jewish people may be proud of its five hundred mule drivers and of its five thousand fusiliers — all of them, from Whitechapel, from Tel-Aviv, New York, Montreal, Buenos Aires and Alexandria. They came from four continents, and one of them from the fifth, Australia. And they did their duty, conscienciously and nobly for the Jewish future.". **VLADIMIR JABOTINSKY ON THE ZION MULE CORPS**

RUSSIA

Berdychev

UKRAINE

Odessa

GALICIA

POLAND

HUNGARY

BATAVIA

Waterloo

ITALY

Dardanelles

Tel-Hai

Umm es Shert

PALESTINE

0   300
Miles

THE JEWS OF AUSTRIA–HUNGARY 1867-1914

Scale: 0 — 100 Miles

1897-1910. Karl Lueger, the Mayor, dismisses Jewish officials and introduces segregation in schools. Anti-Jewish pamphlets, speeches and violence allowed

1885. Schönerer's Linz Programme declares "the removal of all Jewish influences from all sections of public life is indispensable"

1877. Jewish rabbinical college founded

1882. Ritual murder charge made against Jews. Despite aquittals, the charge led to many outbreaks of anti-semitic violence

Despite anti-semitic outbreaks, the Jews of Austria-Hungary played a significant part in the country's intellectual and economic life

Emigration of over a million Jews to the United States

● Towns with large Jewish communities. The number of Jews, and their percentage of the total population, is given for towns with over 8,000 Jews

▨ Area in which over 5,000 Jews died each year through starvation 1880-1914

GALICIA

BUKOVINA

Brody 12,000 70%
Lemberg 57,000 28%
Tarnopol 14,000 41%
Kolomea 19,000 44%
Czernowitz 29,000 33%
Tarnow
Przemysl
Munkacs
Kolozsvar
Cracow 32,000 21%
Zombor
Tizsa-Eszlar
Debreczen
Bekes
Temesvar
Eger ●
Szegedin
Buda ● ● Pest "Judapest" 204,000 23%
Kaposvar
Pressburg 8,000 10%
Brno 9,000 7%
Nagy-Kanizsa
Vienna 175,000 9%
Prague 18,000 8%
Linz ●
Trieste ●

79

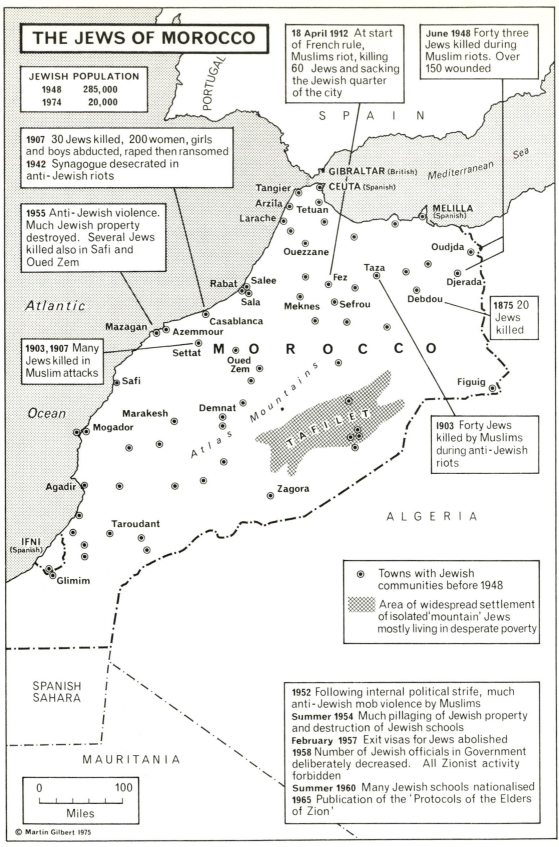

THE JEWS OF MOROCCO

JEWISH POPULATION
1948   285,000
1974   20,000

1907 30 Jews killed, 200 women, girls and boys abducted, raped then ransomed
1942 Synagogue desecrated in anti-Jewish riots

1955 Anti-Jewish violence. Much Jewish property destroyed. Several Jews killed also in Safi and Oued Zem

18 April 1912 At start of French rule, Muslims riot, killing 60 Jews and sacking the Jewish quarter of the city

June 1948 Forty three Jews killed during Muslim riots. Over 150 wounded

PORTUGAL

S P A I N

Mediterranean Sea

GIBRALTAR (British)
Tangier   CEUTA (Spanish)
Arzila   Tetuan
Larache   MELILLA
                                 (Spanish)
Ouezzane   Oudjda

Atlantic   Taza
                Fez   Djerada
Rabat Salee
       Sala   Meknes Sefrou   Debdou
Casablanca   **1875** 20 Jews killed
Mazagan Azemmour
         Settat   M O R O C C O
1903, 1907 Many Jews killed in Muslim attacks
         Oued Zem
Ocean Safi
                                  Figuig
         Marakesh Demnat
         Mogador   *Atlas Mountains* TAFILLET
                                                 1903 Forty Jews killed by Muslims during anti-Jewish riots

Agadir
                   Zagora
                                    A L G E R I A
         Taroudant

IFNI
(Spanish)
      Glimim

⊙ Towns with Jewish communities before 1948

▨ Area of widespread settlement of isolated 'mountain' Jews mostly living in desperate poverty

SPANISH SAHARA

M A U R I T A N I A

1952 Following internal political strife, much anti-Jewish mob violence by Muslims
Summer 1954 Much pillaging of Jewish property and destruction of Jewish schools
February 1957 Exit visas for Jews abolished
1958 Number of Jewish officials in Government deliberately decreased. All Zionist activity forbidden
Summer 1960 Many Jewish schools nationalised
1965 Publication of the 'Protocols of the Elders of Zion'

0   100
    Miles

© Martin Gilbert 1975

Principal Jewish communities by 1914
Other towns with Jewish communities

THE JEWS OF BRITAIN
1660 – 1914

1905. Aliens Act gives immigration officers the right to deport any "undesirable immigrant". Flow of Jews reduced by 40%

THE JEWS IN BRITAIN	
1660	150
1690	400
1734	6,000
1790	26,000
1850	30,000
1882	46,000
1914	300,000

Glasgow 6,500
Edinburgh 1,500

2,000 Newcastle
North Shields
South Shields
Gateshead
Sunderland
West Hartlepool
Stockton
Middlesborough

Hull 1,500

Bradford
Leeds 15,000

Liverpool 5,000
Manchester 25,000
Sheffield

King's Lynn
Norwich
Yarmouth

Wolverhampton
Birmingham 5,500
Coventry
Cambridge
Bedford
Ipswich

1911. Anti-Jewish riots by miners

Cheltenham
Oxford
Stroud
Merthyr
Tredegar
Aberdare
Newport
Bristol
Swansea
Pontypridd
Cardiff
Bath
Reading
London 180,000
Chatham
Canterbury
Ramsgate
Dover

1882-1914. 4 ships a week from Hamburg, 3 from Rotterdam, 3 from Breslau and 1 from Libau bring nearly 300,000 Russian, Galician and Rumanian Jews

Southampton
Portsmouth
Brighton

Exeter
Plymouth
Falmouth

MAIN JEWISH TRADES
Tailoring 40%
Boot & Slipper Trade 12%
Furniture Trade 10%

JEWISH TRADE UNIONS IN 1900:
Tailors, Capmakers, Boot & Shoe Operatives, Cabinet Makers, Cigarette & Tobacco Cutters, Iron & Tin Plate Makers, Brush Makers, Cardboard Box Makers, House Painters & Decorators, Butchers, Poulterers, Bakers.

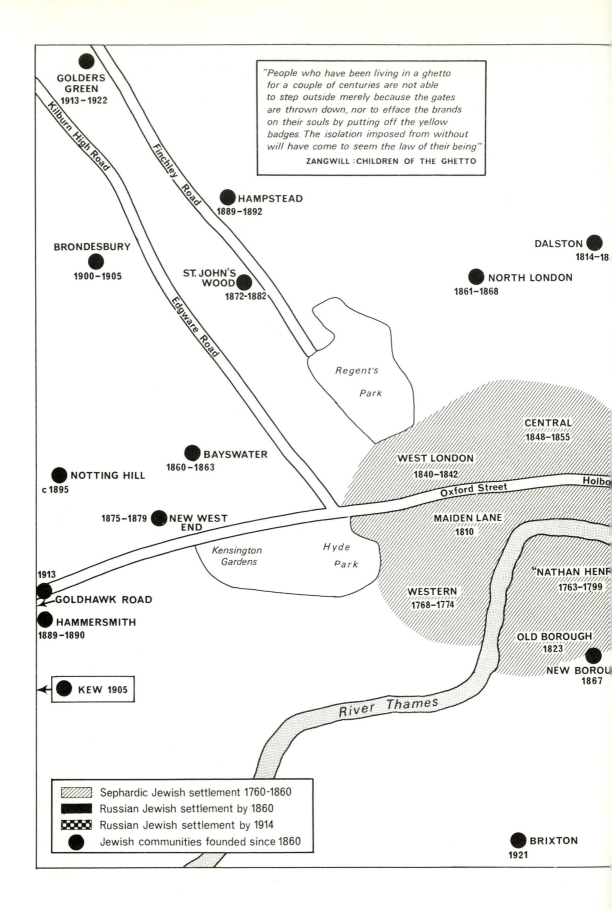

GOLDERS
GREEN
1913-1922

Kilburn High Road

Finchley Road

HAMPSTEAD
1889-1892

DALSTON
1814-18

BRONDESBURY

1900-1905

ST. JOHN'S
WOOD
1872-1882

NORTH LONDON
1861-1868

Edgware Road

Regent's

Park

CENTRAL
1848-1855

BAYSWATER
1860-1863

WEST LONDON
1840-1842

NOTTING HILL

c 1895

Holbo

Oxford Street

1875-1879   NEW WEST
END

MAIDEN LANE
1810

"NATHAN HENR
1763-1799

Kensington
Gardens

Hyde
Park

1913

GOLDHAWK ROAD

WESTERN
1768-1774

HAMMERSMITH

1889-1890

OLD BOROUGH
1823

NEW BOROU
1867

KEW 1905

River Thames

*"People who have been living in a ghetto
for a couple of centuries are not able
to step outside merely because the gates
are thrown down, nor to efface the brands
on their souls by putting off the yellow
badges. The isolation imposed from without
will have come to seem the law of their being"*
ZANGWILL : CHILDREN OF THE GHETTO

Sephardic Jewish settlement 1760-1860
Russian Jewish settlement by 1860
Russian Jewish settlement by 1914
Jewish communities founded since 1860

BRIXTON
1921

NEW SYNAGOGUE (STAMFORD HILL) 1913–1915

FINSBURY PARK

LONDON JEWRY SINCE 1900

Stoke Newington Road

Leytonstone High Road

WEST HAM c1900

Romford Road

WALTHAMSTOW & LEYTON 1902

STOKE NEWINGTON 1887–1903

Kingsland Road

HACKNEY 1881–1897

Victoria Park

Bow Road

THE EAST END

Mile End Road

ditch

Stepney Green

Where two dates are given, the first is of the decision to form a congregation or of the holding of the first regular services; the second date is of the opening of a permanent synagogue

POPLAR c1890

SOUTH EAST LONDON 1899

1880–1914. Over half of the Russian Jews reaching London continued by boat to the USA

London Jewish Population	
1850	18,000
1880	45,000
1900	125,000
1914	180,000
1960	280,000

0   1

Mile

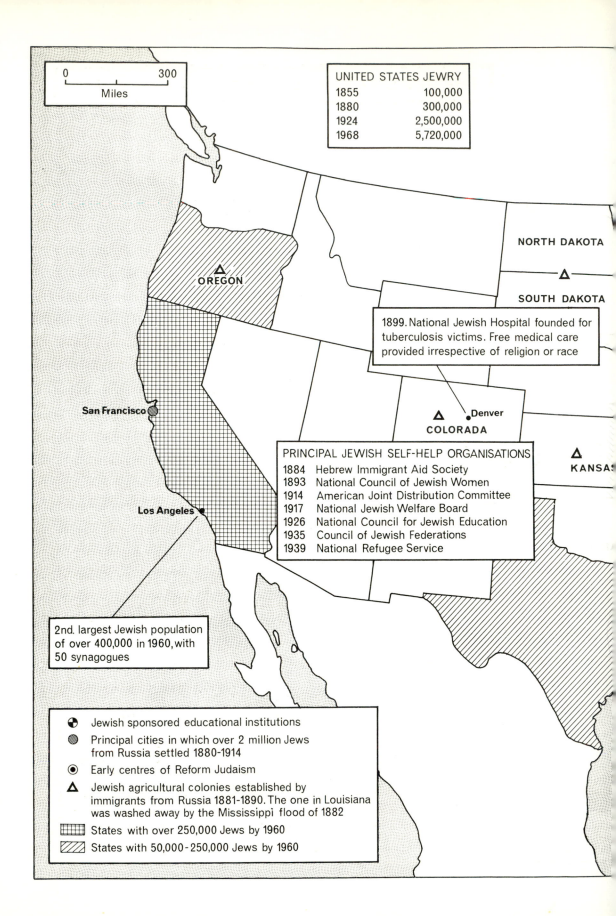

0	300
	Miles

UNITED STATES JEWRY
1855	100,000
1880	300,000
1924	2,500,000
1968	5,720,000

NORTH DAKOTA

SOUTH DAKOTA

1899. National Jewish Hospital founded for tuberculosis victims. Free medical care provided irrespective of religion or race

OREGON

San Francisco

• Denver

COLORADA

KANSAS

PRINCIPAL JEWISH SELF-HELP ORGANISATIONS
1884	Hebrew Immigrant Aid Society
1893	National Council of Jewish Women
1914	American Joint Distribution Committee
1917	National Jewish Welfare Board
1926	National Council for Jewish Education
1935	Council of Jewish Federations
1939	National Refugee Service

Los Angeles •

2nd. largest Jewish population of over 400,000 in 1960, with 50 synagogues

Jewish sponsored educational institutions

Principal cities in which over 2 million Jews from Russia settled 1880-1914

Early centres of Reform Judaism

Jewish agricultural colonies established by immigrants from Russia 1881-1890. The one in Louisiana was washed away by the Mississippi flood of 1882

States with over 250,000 Jews by 1960

States with 50,000-250,000 Jews by 1960

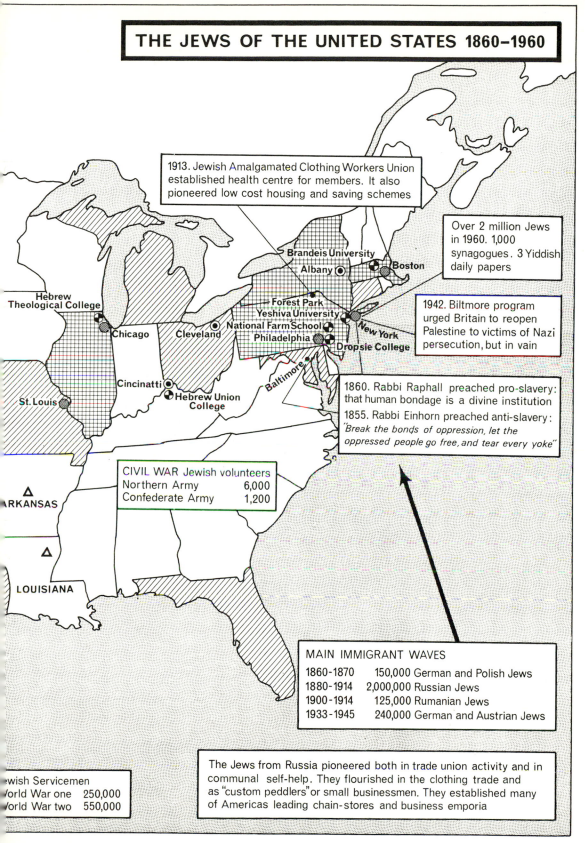

THE JEWS OF THE UNITED STATES 1860–1960

1913. Jewish Amalgamated Clothing Workers Union established health centre for members. It also pioneered low cost housing and saving schemes

Over 2 million Jews in 1960. 1,000 synagogues. 3 Yiddish daily papers

1942. Biltmore program urged Britain to reopen Palestine to victims of Nazi persecution, but in vain

1860. Rabbi Raphall preached pro-slavery: that human bondage is a divine institution

1855. Rabbi Einhorn preached anti-slavery: *"Break the bonds of oppression, let the oppressed people go free, and tear every yoke"*

Brandeis University
Albany
Boston
Hebrew Theological College
Forest Park
Yeshiva University
New York
Chicago
Cleveland
National Farm School
Philadelphia
Dropsie College
Cincinatti
Hebrew Union College
St. Louis
Baltimore

ARKANSAS

LOUISIANA

CIVIL WAR Jewish volunteers
Northern Army   6,000
Confederate Army   1,200

MAIN IMMIGRANT WAVES

Years	Number	Group
1860-1870	150,000	German and Polish Jews
1880-1914	2,000,000	Russian Jews
1900-1914	125,000	Rumanian Jews
1933-1945	240,000	German and Austrian Jews

The Jews from Russia pioneered both in trade union activity and in communal self-help. They flourished in the clothing trade and as "custom peddlers" or small businessmen. They established many of Americas leading chain-stores and business emporia

Jewish Servicemen
World War one   250,000
World War two   550,000

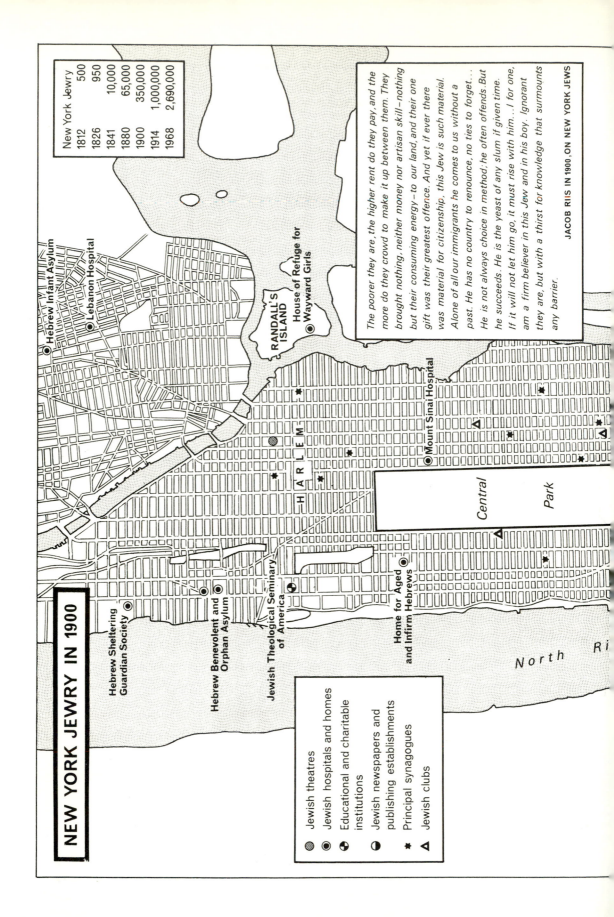

NEW YORK JEWRY IN 1900

New York Jewry	
1812	500
1826	950
1841	10,000
1880	65,000
1900	350,000
1914	1,000,000
1968	2,690,000

The poorer they are, the higher rent do they pay, and the more do they crowd to make it up between them. They brought nothing, neither money nor artisan skill – nothing but their consuming energy – to our land, and their one gift was their greatest offence. And yet if ever there was material for citizenship, this Jew is such material. Alone of all our immigrants he comes to us without a past. He has no country to renounce, no ties to forget... He is not always choice in method; he often offends. But he succeeds. He is the yeast of any slum if given time. If it will not let him go, it must rise with him... I for one, am a firm believer in this Jew and in his boy. Ignorant they are, but with a thirst for knowledge that surmounts any barrier.

JACOB RIIS IN 1900, ON NEW YORK JEWS

Hebrew Infant Asylum

Lebanon Hospital

RANDALL'S ISLAND

House of Refuge for Wayward Girls

HARLEM

Mount Sinai Hospital

Central

Park

Hebrew Sheltering Guardian Society

Hebrew Benevolent and Orphan Asylum

Jewish Theological Seminary of America

Home for Aged and Infirm Hebrews

North Ri

Legend

- ◍ Jewish theatres
- ◉ Jewish hospitals and homes
- ◑ Educational and charitable institutions
- ◐ Jewish newspapers and publishing establishments
- ✳ Principal synagogues
- △ Jewish clubs

By 1900 New York had a larger Jewish population than any other city in the world. It has kept this position ever since

East River

Clara de Hirsch
Home for Working Girls

Hebrew Charities
Building

Hebrew Technical
Institute for Boys

Hebrew Technical School
for Girls

Beth Israel
Hospital

East River

Broadway

Fifth Avenue

Old Jewish
Cemetery

Old Jewish
Cemetery

Broadway

First Synagogue
c.1700

North River

1654	First Jewish settlement
1657	Jews admitted to citizenship
1766	First Jewish prayer book published in English
1825	Influx of German and Polish Jews begins
1879	First Jewish weekly newspaper founded
1881	Influx of Russian Jews begins
1900	Influx of Rumanian and Galician Jews
1902	Anti-semitic riot provoked during a rabbis funeral "by the unwonted spectacle of thousands of aliens"
1933	Influx of German refugees from Nazism begins

In 1904 this area contained 64,000 Jewish families living in less than 6,000 tenements. They had 306 synagogues, 307 schools of religious instruction and 4 theatres. They also gave over a million dollars a year to charity

0   Mile   1

84

JEWISH SETTLEMENT IN PALESTINE 1880 – 1914

Between 1880 and 1914 over sixty thousand Jews entered Palestine, mostly from Russia, Galicia, Rumania and Poland. The victims of persecution and discrimination, they sought a new homeland and a new security under Turkish rule. Many settled on wasteland, sand-dunes and malarial marsh, which they then drained, irrigated and farmed. In 1909 a group of Jews founded the first entirely Jewish town, Tel Aviv, on the sandhills north of Jaffa. The Jews purchased their land piecemeal, from European, Turkish and (principally) Arab landlords, mostly at extremely high prices

Metulla

Yesod Hamaala

Ayelet Hashahar

Ein Zeitim

Mishmar Hayarden

Mahanayim

Safed

Rosh Pina

Acre

Migdal

Kfar Hittim

Sea of Galilee

Haifa

Mizpa

Tiberias

Bnei Yehuda

Sejera

Nazareth

Poriya

Kinneret

Sharona

Deganya

Atlit

Kfar Tavor

Beitanya

Tantura

Shefeiya

Beit Gan

Menahemya

Bat Shelomo

Merhavya

Yavneel

Zikhron Yaakov

Givat Ada

Beisan

Karkur

Nahliel

Jenin

Heftzibah

Gan Shmuel

Hadera

Tulkarm

Kfar Mahal

Nablus

Kfar Sava

Mikve Israel

Ein Hai

Petah Tikvah

Tel Aviv

Ein Ganim

Jaffa

Mahane Yehuda

Nahalat Yehuda

Ben Shemen

Rishon le Zion

Beer Yaakov

Ramla

Ramallah

Nes Ziona

Rehovot

Jericho

Ekron

Hulda

Kfar Uriya

Motza

Gedera

Jerusalem

Hartuv

Beer - Toviya
(Kastinia)

Gaza

Hebron

Ruhama

Beersheba

Jordan

Dead Sea

APPROXIMATE POPULATIONS

1880:	470,000 Arabs
	24,000 Jews
1914:	500,000 Arabs
	90,000 Jews

0	5	10	15

Miles

Between 1880 and 1903 over 25,000 Jews reached Palestine, mostly from Russia, and settled on the land. Between 1904 and 1914 a further 40,000 Jews arrived from eastern Europe, many of whom worked as hired labourers both on the land and in the towns. This 'second' Aliyah formed the first Jewish political parties in Palestine, and laid the foundations of a Hebrew press and modern Hebrew literature

○ Arab towns with few, if any Jewish inhabitants by 1914

◉ Jewish settlements established between 1880 and 1914

● Towns with Jewish as well as Arab populations

© Martin Gilbert

85

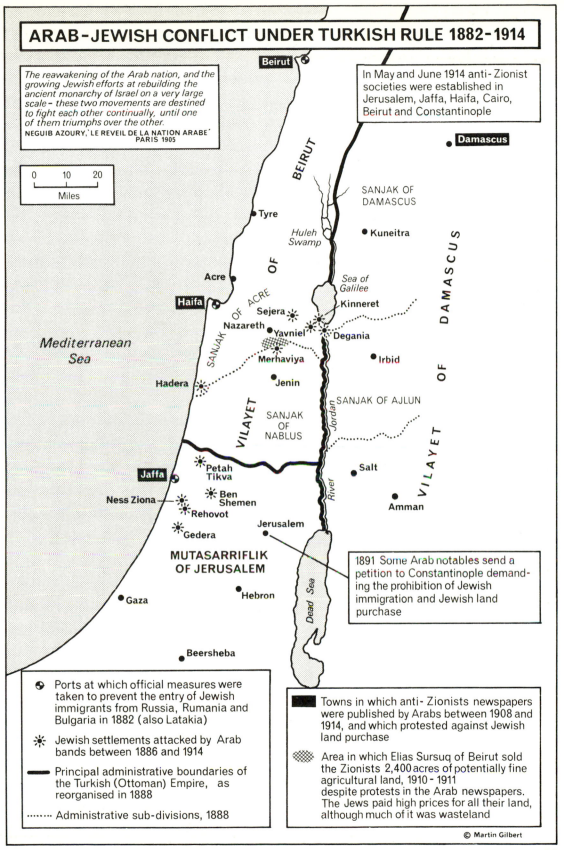

ARAB-JEWISH CONFLICT UNDER TURKISH RULE 1882-1914

The reawakening of the Arab nation, and the growing Jewish efforts at rebuilding the ancient monarchy of Israel on a very large scale – these two movements are destined to fight each other continually, until one of them triumphs over the other.

NEGUIB AZOURY, 'LE REVEIL DE LA NATION ARABE' PARIS 1905

0   10   20
Miles

In May and June 1914 anti-Zionist societies were established in Jerusalem, Jaffa, Haifa, Cairo, Beirut and Constantinople

Beirut

Damascus

BEIRUT

SANJAK OF DAMASCUS

Tyre

Huleh Swamp

Kuneitra

VILAYET   OF   DAMASCUS

Acre

Sea of Galilee

Haifa

SANJAK OF ACRE

Sejera

Kinneret

Nazareth

Yavniel

Degania

Mediterranean Sea

Merhaviya

Irbid

Hadera

Jenin

SANJAK OF AJLUN

VILAYET

SANJAK OF NABLUS

Jordan River

Salt

VILAYET

Jaffa

Petah Tikva

Ness Ziona

Ben Shemen

Rehovot

Amman

Gedera

Jerusalem

MUTASARRIFLIK OF JERUSALEM

1891 Some Arab notables send a petition to Constantinople demanding the prohibition of Jewish immigration and Jewish land purchase

Gaza

Hebron

Dead Sea

Beersheba

⊕ Ports at which official measures were taken to prevent the entry of Jewish immigrants from Russia, Rumania and Bulgaria in 1882 (also Latakia)

☀ Jewish settlements attacked by Arab bands between 1886 and 1914

▬ Principal administrative boundaries of the Turkish (Ottoman) Empire, as reorganised in 1888

······· Administrative sub-divisions, 1888

▮ Towns in which anti-Zionists newspapers were published by Arabs between 1908 and 1914, and which protested against Jewish land purchase

▨ Area in which Elias Sursuq of Beirut sold the Zionists 2,400 acres of potentially fine agricultural land, 1910 - 1911 despite protests in the Arab newspapers. The Jews paid high prices for all their land, although much of it was wasteland

© Martin Gilbert

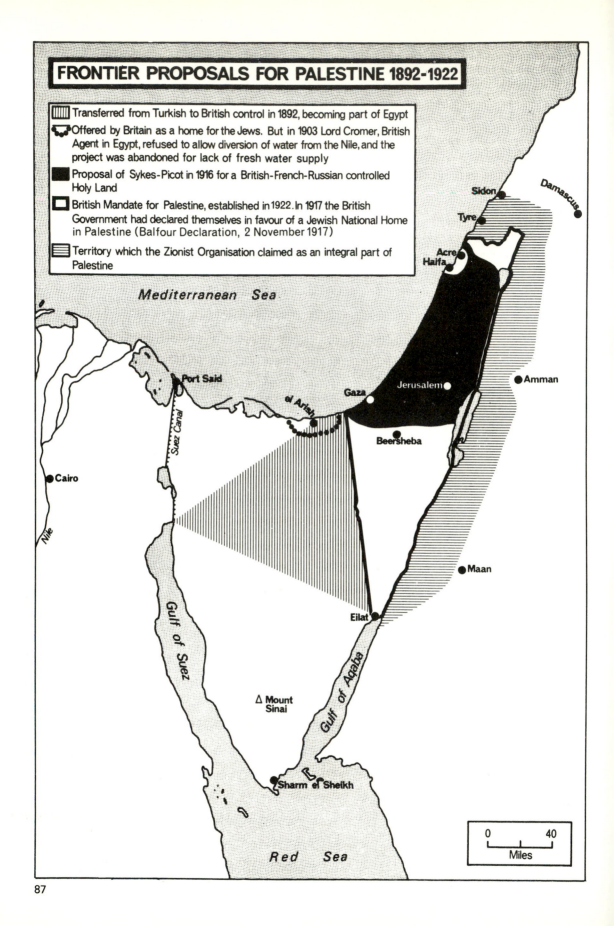

FRONTIER PROPOSALS FOR PALESTINE 1892-1922

Transferred from Turkish to British control in 1892, becoming part of Egypt

Offered by Britain as a home for the Jews. But in 1903 Lord Cromer, British Agent in Egypt, refused to allow diversion of water from the Nile, and the project was abandoned for lack of fresh water supply

Proposal of Sykes-Picot in 1916 for a British-French-Russian controlled Holy Land

British Mandate for Palestine, established in 1922. In 1917 the British Government had declared themselves in favour of a Jewish National Home in Palestine (Balfour Declaration, 2 November 1917)

Territory which the Zionist Organisation claimed as an integral part of Palestine

Damascus

Sidon

Tyre

Acre
Haifa

Mediterranean Sea

Port Said

el Arish

Gaza

Jerusalem

Amman

Beersheba

Suez Canal

Cairo

Nile

Maan

Gulf of Suez

Gulf of Aqaba

Eilat

△ Mount
Sinai

Sharm el Sheikh

Red Sea

0   40
Miles

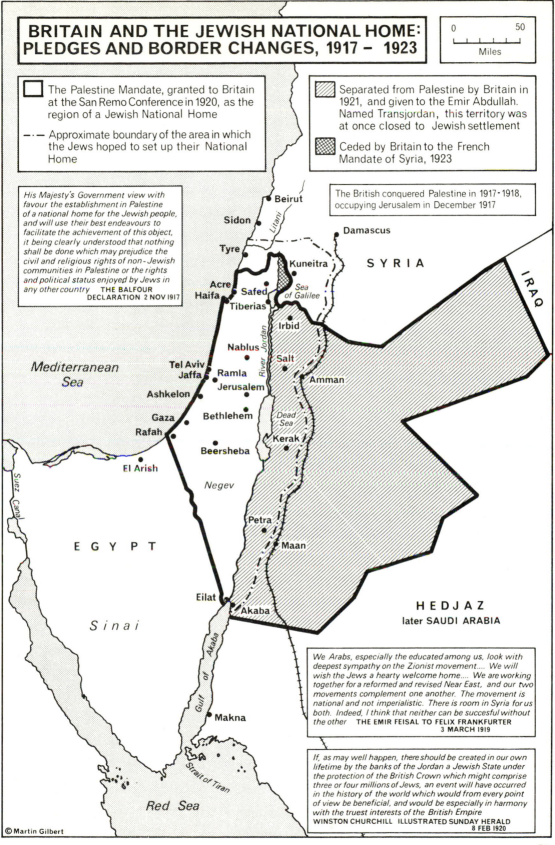

BRITAIN AND THE JEWISH NATIONAL HOME: PLEDGES AND BORDER CHANGES, 1917 – 1923

0   50
Miles

☐ The Palestine Mandate, granted to Britain at the San Remo Conference in 1920, as the region of a Jewish National Home

–·– Approximate boundary of the area in which the Jews hoped to set up their National Home

▨ Separated from Palestine by Britain in 1921, and given to the Emir Abdullah. Named Transjordan, this territory was at once closed to Jewish settlement

▩ Ceded by Britain to the French Mandate of Syria, 1923

His Majesty's Government view with favour the establishment in Palestine of a national home for the Jewish people, and will use their best endeavours to facilitate the achievement of this object, it being clearly understood that nothing shall be done which may prejudice the civil and religious rights of non-Jewish communities in Palestine or the rights and political status enjoyed by Jews in any other country **THE BALFOUR DECLARATION 2 NOV 1917**

The British conquered Palestine in 1917-1918, occupying Jerusalem in December 1917

Beirut

Sidon

Damascus

Tyre

SYRIA

Kuneitra

Acre
Haifa
Safed
Tiberias
Sea of Galilee

Irbid

IRAQ

Nablus
Salt

Mediterranean Sea

Tel Aviv
Jaffa
Ramla
Jerusalem

River Jordan

Amman

Ashkelon

Bethlehem

Dead Sea

Gaza
Rafah

Kerak

Beersheba

Negev

El Arish

Suez Canal

Petra

EGYPT

Maan

HEDJAZ
later SAUDI ARABIA

Sinai

Eilat
Akaba

Gulf of Akaba

We Arabs, especially the educated among us, look with deepest sympathy on the Zionist movement.... We will wish the Jews a hearty welcome home.... We are working together for a reformed and revised Near East, and our two movements complement one another. The movement is national and not imperialistic. There is room in Syria for us both. Indeed, I think that neither can be succesful without the other **THE EMIR FEISAL TO FELIX FRANKFURTER 3 MARCH 1919**

Makna

If, as may well happen, there should be created in our own lifetime by the banks of the Jordan a Jewish State under the protection of the British Crown which might comprise three or four millions of Jews, an event will have occurred in the history of the world which would from every point of view be beneficial, and would be especially in harmony with the truest interests of the British Empire **WINSTON CHURCHILL ILLUSTRATED SUNDAY HERALD 8 FEB 1920**

Strait of Tiran

Red Sea

© Martin Gilbert

88

JEWISH SOLDIERS 1914–1918

RUSSIA
650,000
100,000

OTTOMAN EMPIRE
18,000
1,000

Jerusalem

Gallipoli

Tannenberg

RUMANIA
38,000
900

BULGARIA
12,500
1,000

SERBIA
1,200
250

GREECE
4,400
300

AUSTRIA - HUNGARY
320,000
40,000

Caporetto

ITALY
6,000
500

GERMANY
100,000
12,000

BELGIUM
1,000
125

Verdun

Ypres

SWITZERLAND

HOLLAND

DENMARK

FRANCE
55,000
9,500

GREAT BRITAIN
50,000
8,600

UNITED STATES
250,000
3,400

SPAIN

300
Miles
0

9,500	Number of Jews serving in national armies, making a total of 1,500,000
2,000	Jewish war dead: total 140,000
▨	Principal fighting areas
▧	Neutral countries

89

EUROPEAN ANTI-SEMITISM 1917–1933

13,000 to Vladivostok and Harbin

1918. 900 Jews forced into the sea and drowned

1932. Ritual murder charge. Anti-Jewish riots

1917. Jewish schools and synagogues destroyed by fire

1918. Jewish elders massacred

German Foreign Minister murdered: "Knock off Walter Rathenau the dirty god-damned Jewish sow."

1920–1933. Hitler preaches anti-semitism

1933–1939. Small anti-semitic movements culminate in local anti-Jewish violence in imitation of Germany

Emancipation granted in 1930 but withdrawn by Franco in 1938

WHITE RUSSIA

UKRAINE

Odessa

Yalta

Sebastopol

POLAND

Lemberg

Auschwitz

Cracow

CZECHOSLOVAKIA

RUMANIA

BULGARIA

Kavalla

HUNGARY

AUSTRIA

YUGOSLAVIA

Salonika

GREECE

TURKEY

PALESTINE
British Mandate 1920–1947

Berlin 1922

Munich

GREAT BRITAIN

FRANCE

SPAIN

To U.S.A. and Latin America

Area of anti-Jewish atrocities 1917–1921, mostly by anti-Bolshevik Russian armies. Over 100,000 Jews killed

The Flight of Jews 1917–1921

Towns in which specially organised Jewish Militias warded off anti-Jewish attacks 1918–1921

Countries in which Jewish rights were restricted, and anti-semitism flourished

THE CRIMEA 800 BC-1960

Jewish communities 500BC-500AD

Coast along which the Jews were
protected by the Genoese 1263-1400

Karaite Jewish communities by 1300AD

Principal Jewish communities during
Turkish rule 1475-1783

Ashkenazi Jewish communities after
the Russian conquest of 1783

By 1944 the Germans had murdered
most of the 40,000 Ashkenazi and
10,000 Karaites of the Crimea. 300
Karaites survived

RULERS OF THE CRIMEA

800BC	Celts
600BC	Scythians
400BC	Greeks
1AD	Romans
250	Goths
376	Huns
700	Jewish Khazars
1016	Byzantine Greeks
1237	Mongols(north)
1263	Genoese(south)
1475	Ottoman Turks
1783	Russians
1941	Germans
1944	Russians

14,000 Jews in 1905. 9 synagogues,
3 schools, a house of refuge for
travellers and a Jewish hospital

1893-1917. Jews forbidden
to live in Yalta, where Tsar
had his summer palace

1928 Soviet plan to set up
Jewish agricultural settlements
in the barren areas. Thousands
of Jews arrived before the
plan was abandoned

Jews excluded, although the Crimea was
in the Pale of Settlement 1835-1917

1854-1856 Jews serve in the Russian
Army during the Crimean War
against Britain, France and Turkey

Sea of Azov

Putrid Sea

Black Sea

Phanagoria

Kertch

Yenikale

Theodosia (Kaffa)

Karasu-bazar

Kale

Simferopol

Bakhchisaray

Eupatoria (Koslov)

Sevastopol

Balaklava

Yalta

Perekop

Armyansk

0   20
Miles

BIROBIDJAN: A SOVIET EXPERIMENT, 1928 - 1985

1928 The Soviet Government establish a Jewish National District (okrug).
1934 Birobidjan becomes a Jewish Autonomous Region (oblast).
1939 East European refugees fleeing from Nazism not allowed to settle in the region.
1941 30,000 Jews out of a total population of 114,000.
1948 Up to 20,000 more Jews reach the Region.
1958 Khruschev admits failure of the Region's aim of 300,000 Jews, and blames the failure on 'Jewish individualism'.
1959 Census reveals only 14,269 Jews in Birobidjan. 39% give Yiddish as their mother tongue.
1985 Less than 12,000 Jews in the region, forming only one fifteenth of the total population. Yiddish spoken by only 17% of Jews.

THE SOVIET UNION

Khabarovsk

- Kuldur
- Bira
- Birobidjan
- Smidovich
- Birakan
- Obluchye
- Pashkovo
- Birofeld

B I R O B I D J A N

- Ermakovski
- Radde
- Leninskoe
- Pompeyevka
- Bidzhan

River Amur

River Ussuri

C H I N A

In 1941, at the height of the Region's activity, it had 128 elementary schools with Yiddish as the language of instruction, a Museum of Jewish Culture, a daily Yiddish newspaper, a medical school, a music school and 27 Jewish collective and state farms.

0 20 40 miles	
0 25 50 km	

The Jewish Autonomous Region.
Main road link between Moscow and Vladivostok.
Trans-Siberian railway.
Marshland.

THE SOVIET UNION

- Leningrad
- Moscow
- Kiev
- ISRAEL

BIROBIDJAN

Vladivostok

CHINA

© Martin Gilbert 1976

	JEWS ARRIVING	JEWS LEAVING WITHIN A YEAR
1928	950	600
1929	1,875	1,125
1930	2,560	1,000
1931	3,250	725
1932-3	11,000	8,000

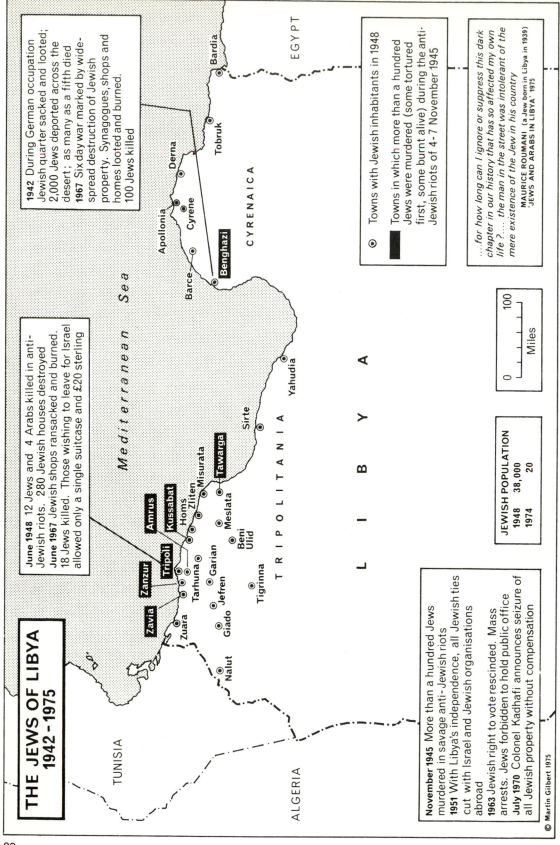

THE JEWS OF LIBYA 1942–1975

1942 During German occupation Jewish quarter sacked and looted; 2,000 Jews deported across the desert; as many as a fifth died **1967** Six day war marked by widespread destruction of Jewish property. Synagogues, shops and homes looted and burned. 100 Jews killed

June 1948 12 Jews and 4 Arabs killed in anti-Jewish riots. 280 Jewish houses destroyed **June 1967** Jewish shops ransacked and burned. 18 Jews killed. Those wishing to leave for Israel allowed only a single suitcase and £20 sterling

November 1945 More than a hundred Jews murdered in savage anti-Jewish riots **1951** With Libya's independence, all Jewish ties cut with Israel and Jewish organisations abroad **1963** Jewish right to vote rescinded. Mass arrests. Jews forbidden to hold public office **July 1970** Colonel Kadhafi announces seizure of all Jewish property without compensation

⊙ Towns with Jewish inhabitants in 1948

■ Towns in which more than a hundred Jews were murdered (some tortured first, some burnt alive) during the anti-Jewish riots of 4–7 November 1945

...for how long can I ignore or suppress this dark chapter in our history that has so affected my own life ?.... the man in the street was intolerant of the mere existence of the Jew in his country
MAURICE ROUMANI (a Jew born in Libya in 1939)
'JEWS AND ARABS IN LIBYA' 1975

JEWISH POPULATION	
1948	38,000
1974	20

0   100
Miles

EGYPT

CYRENAICA

Bardia
Tobruk
Derna
Apollonia
Cyrene
Barce
Benghazi

Mediterranean Sea

TRIPOLITANIA

LIBYA

Yahudia
Sirte
Misurata
Zliten
Homs
Kussabat
Meslata
Amrus
Tawarga
Zanzur
Tripoli
Zavia
Tarhuna
Garian
Beni Ulid
Jefren
Tigrinna
Zuara
Giado
Nalut

TUNISIA

ALGERIA

© Martin Gilbert 1975

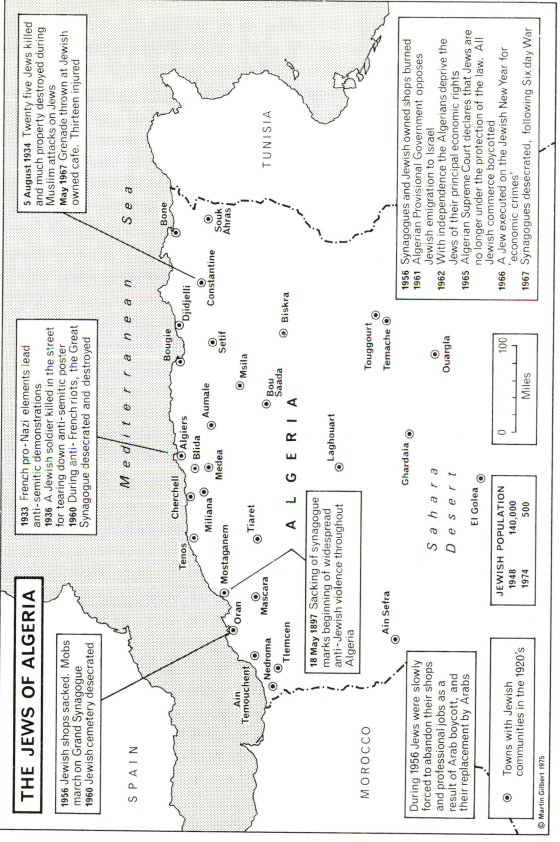

THE JEWS OF ALGERIA

1956 Jewish shops sacked. Mobs march on Grand Synagogue
1960 Jewish cemetery desecrated

1933 French pro-Nazi elements lead anti-semitic demonstrations
1936 A Jewish soldier killed in the street for tearing down anti-semitic poster
1960 During anti-French riots, the Great Synagogue desecrated and destroyed

5 August 1934 Twenty five Jews killed and much property destroyed during Muslim attacks on Jews
May 1967 Grenade thrown at Jewish owned cafe. Thirteen injured

1956 Synagogues and Jewish owned shops burned
1961 Algerian Provisional Government opposes Jewish emigration to Israel
1962 With independence the Algerians deprive the Jews of their principal economic rights
1965 Algerian Supreme Court declares that Jews are no longer under the protection of the law. All Jewish commerce boycotted
1966 A Jew executed on the Jewish New Year for 'economic crimes'
1967 Synagogues desecrated, following Six day War

18 May 1897 Sacking of synagogue marks beginning of widespread anti-Jewish violence throughout Algeria

During 1956 Jews were slowly forced to abandon their shops and professional jobs as a result of Arab boycott, and their replacement by Arabs

SPAIN

Mediterranean Sea

TUNISIA

MOROCCO

A L G E R I A

Sahara Desert

Bone
Souk Ahras
Constantine
Djidjelli
Bougie
Biskra
Setif
Msila
Bou Saada
Aumale
Touggourt
Temache
Ouargla
Algiers
Blida
Medea
Miliana
Cherchell
Tenos
Mostaganem
Tiaret
Mascara
Oran
Nedroma
Tlemcen
Ain Temouchent
Ain Sefra
Laghouart
Ghardaia
El Golea

JEWISH POPULATION	
1948	140,000
1974	500

0 — Miles — 100

⊙ Towns with Jewish communities in the 1920's

© Martin Gilbert 1975

94

THE PERSECUTION OF THE JEWS OF GERMANY IN THE FIRST FIVE YEARS OF NAZI RULE 1933 - 1938

9 March 1933. First anti-Jewish riots in Berlin.
1 April 1933. All Jewish shops in Berlin boycotted.
10 May 1933. In Berlin the Nazis hold a public burning of books written by Jewish and other authors.
October 1933. All hospitals in Berlin declared "free" of Jewish doctors. These doctors could find no other hospital work.

30 January 1933. Hitler becomes the Chancellor of Germany. Many Jews arrested, ill-treated, and tortured.
15 September 1935. The Nuremberg Laws make the Jews second class citizens, and lead to their being driven from public and professional life.
9 November 1938. 191 synagogues set on fire throughout Germany. Over 2,000 Jews murdered in the camps.
15 November 1938. All German schools closed to German Jewish children.

North Sea

Baltic Sea

Esterwegen

Sachsenhausen

1933 - 1939. Of Germany's 525,000 Jews in 1933, over 280,000 emigrated or escaped by 1939.

13 March 1933. All Jewish lawyers and judges expelled from the law courts.

Berlin
Columbia Haus

Braunschweig

Buchenwald

THURINGIA

Breslau

1933. The first Province to eliminate Jews from all official and professional positions.

Nuremberg

FRANCONIA

13 March 1933. Jewish owned shops ransacked and destroyed.

Dachau

Munich

10 August 1938. The synagogue destroyed.

1935. 100,000 German children swear "eternal enmity" to the Jews.

9 June 1938. Synagogue destroyed.

—·— The borders of Germany, 1919 - 1937.

······· Other European borders.

From 1933, "Jews not wanted" signs were put up throughout Germany on shops, cafes, sports stadiums, and on roads leading into towns and villages. In some towns, all Jewish names were scratched off war memorials of the first world war. The savage anti-Jewish propaganda of the "Stürmer" magazine was in public display cases, and within six years, the 2,000 year old Jewish community was turned into a community of outlaws who could expect nothing but harassment and persecution.

Concentration camps set up on German soil by 1938.

Among the many indignities forced upon the Jews was a revival of the medieval practice of making all Jews wear a yellow "Star of David" on their clothing.

© Martin Gilbert 1978

95

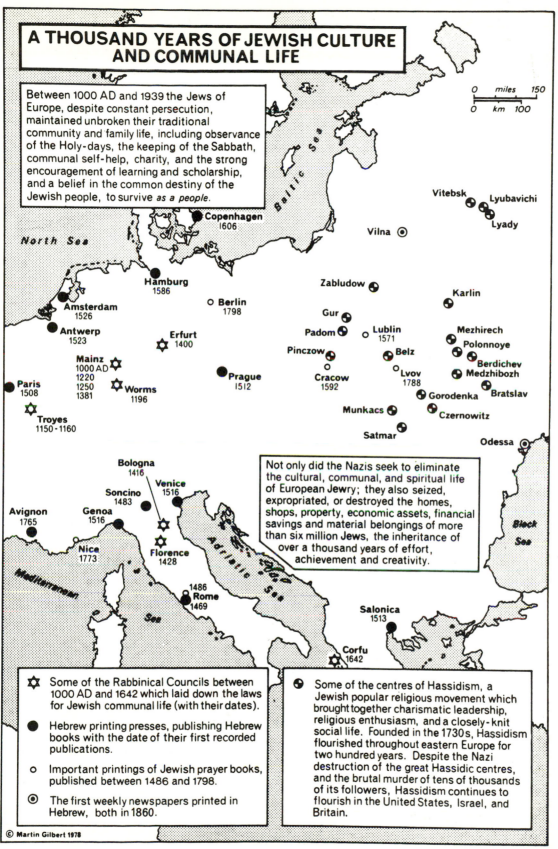

A THOUSAND YEARS OF JEWISH CULTURE AND COMMUNAL LIFE

Between 1000 AD and 1939 the Jews of Europe, despite constant persecution, maintained unbroken their traditional community and family life, including observance of the Holy-days, the keeping of the Sabbath, communal self-help, charity, and the strong encouragement of learning and scholarship, and a belief in the common destiny of the Jewish people, to survive *as a people.*

Not only did the Nazis seek to eliminate the cultural, communal, and spiritual life of European Jewry; they also seized, expropriated, or destroyed the homes, shops, property, economic assets, financial savings and material belongings of more than six million Jews, the inheritance of over a thousand years of effort, achievement and creativity.

Baltic Sea

North Sea

Vitebsk
Lyubavichi
Lyady

Vilna ◉

Copenhagen
1606

Zabludow
Karlin

Hamburg
1586

Gur
Mezhirech
Polonnoye

Berlin
1798

Padom
Lublin
1571
Berdichev

Amsterdam
1526

Erfurt
1400

Pinczow
Belz
Medzhibozh

Antwerp
1523

Mainz
1000 AD
1220
1250
1381

Worms
1196

Prague
1512

Cracow
1592

Lvov
1788

Gorodenka
Bratslav

Paris
1508

Troyes
1150-1160

Munkacs
Czernowitz

Satmar

Odessa ◎

Bologna
1416

Venice
1516

Black Sea

Soncino
1483

Genoa
1516

Avignon
1765

Adriatic Sea

Nice
1773

Florence
1428

Mediterranean Sea

1486
Rome
1469

Salonica
1513

Corfu
1642

✡ Some of the Rabbinical Councils between 1000 AD and 1642 which laid down the laws for Jewish communal life (with their dates).

● Hebrew printing presses, publishing Hebrew books with the date of their first recorded publications.

○ Important printings of Jewish prayer books, published between 1486 and 1798.

◉ The first weekly newspapers printed in Hebrew, both in 1860.

✤ Some of the centres of Hassidism, a Jewish popular religious movement which brought together charismatic leadership, religious enthusiasm, and a closely-knit social life. Founded in the 1730s, Hassidism flourished throughout eastern Europe for two hundred years. Despite the Nazi destruction of the great Hassidic centres, and the brutal murder of tens of thousands of its followers, Hassidism continues to flourish in the United States, Israel, and Britain.

© Martin Gilbert 1978

THE FLIGHT FROM GERMAN PERSECUTION 1933-1941

SOVIET UNION

250,000

BALTIC STATES

WHITE RUSSIA

UKRAINE

BESSARABIA

POLAND

GALICIA

SLOVAKIA

HUNGARY

RUMANIA

BULGARIA

GREECE

500

YUGOSLAVIA

7,000

CZECHO

AUSTRIA

ITALY

SWEDEN

DENMARK

7,000

Hamburg 3,200

71,000
30,000
25,000
20,000
8,000
6,000
2,500

HOLLAND

BELGIUM

25,000

SWITZERLAND

12,000

Marseilles

FRANCE

3,000

15,000

SPAIN

Bilbao

Vigo

PORTUGAL

Lisbon

Oran

Casablanca

GREAT BRITAIN

ISLE OF MAN

Liverpool

London

To North and South America

PALESTINE British Mandate

Beirut

1941. 600 illegal immigrants

Jews reaching Palestine 1933-44 from :-

Poland	12,000	Yugoslavia	800
Rumania	8,000	Lithuania	600
Germany	8,000	USSR	600
Czechoslovakia	6,000	Italy	500
Hungary	3,000	France	300
Bulgaria	3,000	Holland	200
Greece	1,000	Latvia	100

Greater Germany August 1939

Refugees 1933-1941

Ships with Jewish refugees whom the British Government refused to admit to Palestine. These ships were not allowed to land their human cargoes and sank. In all 600 Jews were drowned

Ports through which 370,000 Jews fled to the Americas, 240,000 of them to the United States

Rail and river routes by which 90,000 Jews reached Palestine, many entering illegally despite the British refusal to admit more than 75,000

1940 British Government interns 30,000 German and Austrian Jewish refugees as "enemy aliens"

1944. 8,000 Jewish children saved from death by being hidden in convents and private houses

0   200
Miles

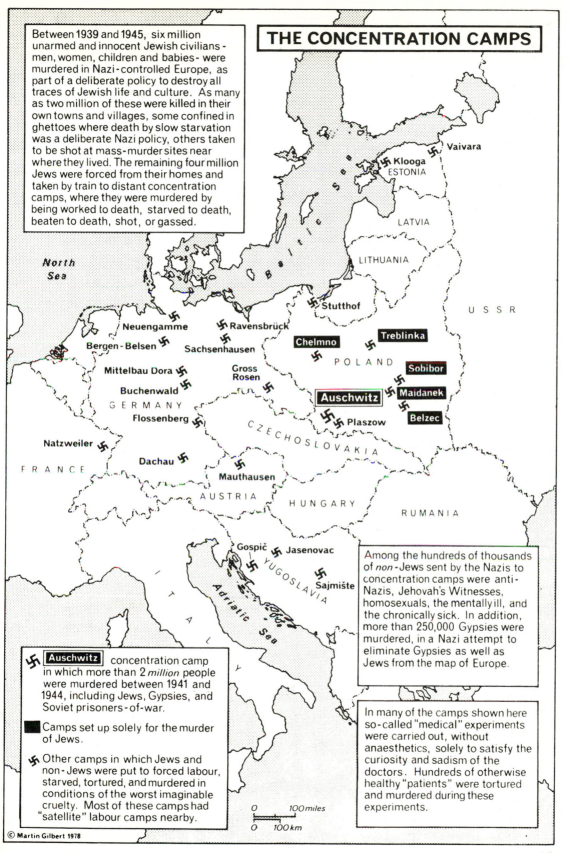

THE CONCENTRATION CAMPS

Between 1939 and 1945, six million unarmed and innocent Jewish civilians - men, women, children and babies - were murdered in Nazi-controlled Europe, as part of a deliberate policy to destroy all traces of Jewish life and culture. As many as two million of these were killed in their own towns and villages, some confined in ghettoes where death by slow starvation was a deliberate Nazi policy, others taken to be shot at mass-murder sites near where they lived. The remaining four million Jews were forced from their homes and taken by train to distant concentration camps, where they were murdered by being worked to death, starved to death, beaten to death, shot, or gassed.

Among the hundreds of thousands of *non*-Jews sent by the Nazis to concentration camps were anti-Nazis, Jehovah's Witnesses, homosexuals, the mentally ill, and the chronically sick. In addition, more than 250,000 Gypsies were murdered, in a Nazi attempt to eliminate Gypsies as well as Jews from the map of Europe.

Auschwitz concentration camp in which more than 2 *million* people were murdered between 1941 and 1944, including Jews, Gypsies, and Soviet prisoners-of-war.

Camps set up solely for the murder of Jews.

Other camps in which Jews and non-Jews were put to forced labour, starved, tortured, and murdered in conditions of the worst imaginable cruelty. Most of these camps had "satellite" labour camps nearby.

In many of the camps shown here so-called "medical" experiments were carried out, without anaesthetics, solely to satisfy the curiosity and sadism of the doctors. Hundreds of otherwise healthy "patients" were tortured and murdered during these experiments.

© Martin Gilbert 1978

North Sea

Baltic Sea

Vaivara

Klooga
ESTONIA

LATVIA

LITHUANIA

U S S R

Stutthof

Neuengamme
Ravensbrück
Bergen-Belsen
Sachsenhausen
Mittelbau Dora
Gross Rosen
Buchenwald
G E R M A N Y
Flossenberg
Natzweiler
Dachau
F R A N C E
Mauthausen
A U S T R I A

Chelmno
Treblinka
P O L A N D
Sobibor
Auschwitz
Maidanek
Belzec
Plaszow
C Z E C H O S L O V A K I A

H U N G A R Y

R U M A N I A

Gospič
Jasenovac
Y U G O S L A V I A
Sajmište

I T A L Y
Adriatic Sea

0   100 miles
0   100 km

JEWS UNDER GERMAN RULE 1933-1941

DENMARK

North Sea

Baltic Sea

● Stettin

HOLLAND

BELGIUM

F R A N C E

SAAR

BADEN

SWITZERLAND

1933-1941 Of Germany's 525,000 Jews over 250,000 emigrated or escaped.

April 1933 Boycott of all Jewish shops

1933 First province to eliminate Jews from all official and professional posts

● Berlin

October 1933 All hospitals declared "free" of Jewish doctors

● Buchenwald

THURINGIA

1935 100,000 German children swear "eternal enmity" to the Jews

Nuremberg ●

FRANCONIA

Dachau ●

● Munich

A U S T R I A

I T A L Y

⊕ Theresienstadt

● Prague

PROTECTORATE OF BOHEMIA AND MORAVIA

Vienna ●

CROA

1940 9,000 Jews expelled to camps in southern France

The Jewish contribution to German cultural and scientific life was greater than to any other European country. By turning the Jews into second-class citizens after 1933, driving them from Germany and seeking to murder those who remained, the Germans cut themselves off from a rich source of their own achievements. A third of Germany's Nobel Prize winners were Jews; among the refugees were a further six who won the prize in their new homeland

33 Hitler becomes German Chancellor
35 Jews made second class citizens by the Nuremberg Laws and driven from public and professional life
38 191 synagogues burned. 20,000 Jews sent to Dachau and Buchenwald concentration camps
40 20,000 Berlin Jews pressed into forced labour battalions
41 Jews forbidden to leave "Greater Germany"

- - - The German frontiers in 1933
→ The expulsion of Jews in 1940
▬▬ The frontiers of Greater Germany in December 1941
⊕ Ghettoes established by the Germans 1939-1942. All the restrictions of the medieval ghettoes were enforced with an added savagery. Food was restricted, curfews enforced and severe overcrowding led to mass starvation. At one time there were 450,000 Jews in the Warsaw and 200,000 in the Lublin ghettoes, forced to live as many as ten to a small room

Riga

REICHSKOMMISSARIAT

MEMEL

Königsberg

EAST PRUSSIA

Vilna

P R U S S I A

OSTLAND

Bialystok

Minsk

Warsaw

WARTHELAND

G E N E R A L

Lodz

Lublin
LUBLINLAND

1939 Planned by the Germans as a reservation for 400,000 Jews. The Jews were to do agricultural work under German supervision 100,000 Jews were deported from Germany and Poland in 4 months. 20,000 died of exposure and starvation

REICHSKOMMISSARIAT

Czestochowa

S I L E S I A

Sosnowiec

G O V E R N M E N T

Cracow

Stryzow

Brody

Lvov

UKRAINE

S L O V A K I A

RUMANIA

1938 German annexation leads to many Jewish suicides

H U N G A R Y

"The departure from Germany of so many writers, artists, musicians, and political leaders had created for the moment a kind of vacuum, for whatever may have been the shortcomings of the Democratic parties, they numbered among their following the intellectual life of the capital and nearly all that was original and stimulating in the world of art and letters"
1933 BRITISH AMBASSADOR SIR H. RUMBOLD
FROM BERLIN

Among the many indignities forced upon the Jews was a revival of the medieval practice of making all Jews wear a yellow "Star of David" on their clothing

0   100
Miles

THE SEARCH FOR SAFETY 1933-1945

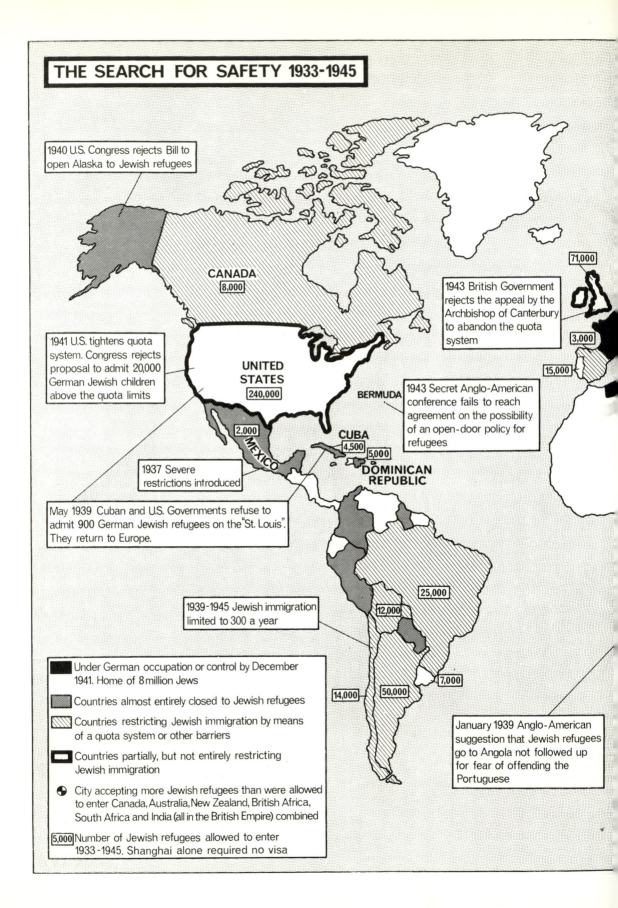

1940 U.S. Congress rejects Bill to open Alaska to Jewish refugees

CANADA
8,000

1943 British Government rejects the appeal by the Archbishop of Canterbury to abandon the quota system

71,000

3,000

15,000

1941 U.S. tightens quota system. Congress rejects proposal to admit 20,000 German Jewish children above the quota limits

UNITED STATES
240,000

BERMUDA

1943 Secret Anglo-American conference fails to reach agreement on the possibility of an open-door policy for refugees

MEXICO
2,000

CUBA
4,500

5,000

DOMINICAN REPUBLIC

1937 Severe restrictions introduced

May 1939 Cuban and U.S. Governments refuse to admit 900 German Jewish refugees on the "St. Louis". They return to Europe.

1939-1945 Jewish immigration limited to 300 a year

25,000

12,000

7,000

14,000

50,000

January 1939 Anglo-American suggestion that Jewish refugees go to Angola not followed up for fear of offending the Portuguese

■ Under German occupation or control by December 1941. Home of 8 million Jews

▨ Countries almost entirely closed to Jewish refugees

▨ Countries restricting Jewish immigration by means of a quota system or other barriers

□ Countries partially, but not entirely restricting Jewish immigration

● City accepting more Jewish refugees than were allowed to enter Canada, Australia, New Zealand, British Africa, South Africa and India (all in the British Empire) combined

5,000 Number of Jewish refugees allowed to enter 1933-1945. Shanghai alone required no visa

1943 U.S. State Department rejects Swedish proposal for joint rescue of 20,000 Jewish children from Germany

Closed to European refugees

U. S. S. R.
250,000

90,000

JEWISH AUTONOMOUS BIROBIDJAN (U.S.S.R)

CHINA
5,000

JAPAN
2,000

Shanghai
25,000

NGOLA

8,000

MAURITIUS
1,750

AUSTRALIA
9,000

933-1935 Unrestricted immigration. Then almost no Jews allowed n 1936-1945

Jews deported by the British from Palestine while seeking "illegal entry". They were allowed to enter Palestine in 1945

"They that sow in tears
  Shall reap in joy.
He that goeth forth and weepeth,
  Bearing precious seed,
Shall doubtless come again with rejoicing
  Bringing his sheaves with him"

PSALM 126

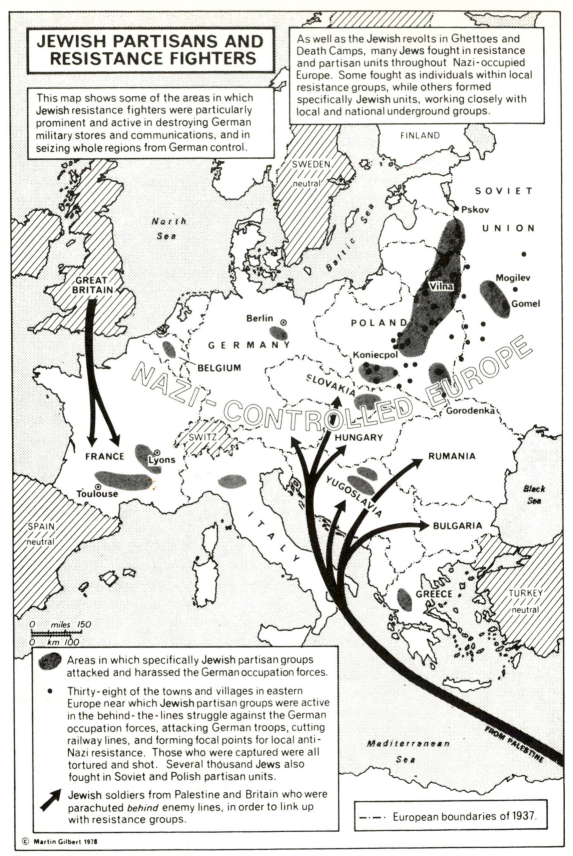

JEWISH PARTISANS AND RESISTANCE FIGHTERS

As well as the Jewish revolts in Ghettoes and Death Camps, many Jews fought in resistance and partisan units throughout Nazi-occupied Europe. Some fought as individuals within local resistance groups, while others formed specifically Jewish units, working closely with local and national underground groups.

This map shows some of the areas in which Jewish resistance fighters were particularly prominent and active in destroying German military stores and communications, and in seizing whole regions from German control.

FINLAND

SWEDEN
neutral

North Sea

Baltic Sea

SOVIET

UNION

Pskov

GREAT
BRITAIN

Vilna

Mogilev

Gomel

Berlin ◎

GERMANY

POLAND

NAZI-CONTROLLED EUROPE

BELGIUM

Koniecpol

SLOVAKIA

SWITZ

HUNGARY

Gorodenka

FRANCE

Lyons

RUMANIA

Toulouse

YUGOSLAVIA

Black
Sea

SPAIN
neutral

ITALY

BULGARIA

GREECE

TURKEY
neutral

FROM PALESTINE

Mediterranean
Sea

0   miles 150
0   km 100

▨ Areas in which specifically Jewish partisan groups attacked and harassed the German occupation forces.

• Thirty-eight of the towns and villages in eastern Europe near which Jewish partisan groups were active in the behind-the-lines struggle against the German occupation forces, attacking German troops, cutting railway lines, and forming focal points for local anti-Nazi resistance. Those who were captured were all tortured and shot. Several thousand Jews also fought in Soviet and Polish partisan units.

➤ Jewish soldiers from Palestine and Britain who were parachuted *behind* enemy lines, in order to link up with resistance groups.

— ・ — European boundaries of 1937.

© Martin Gilbert 1978

101

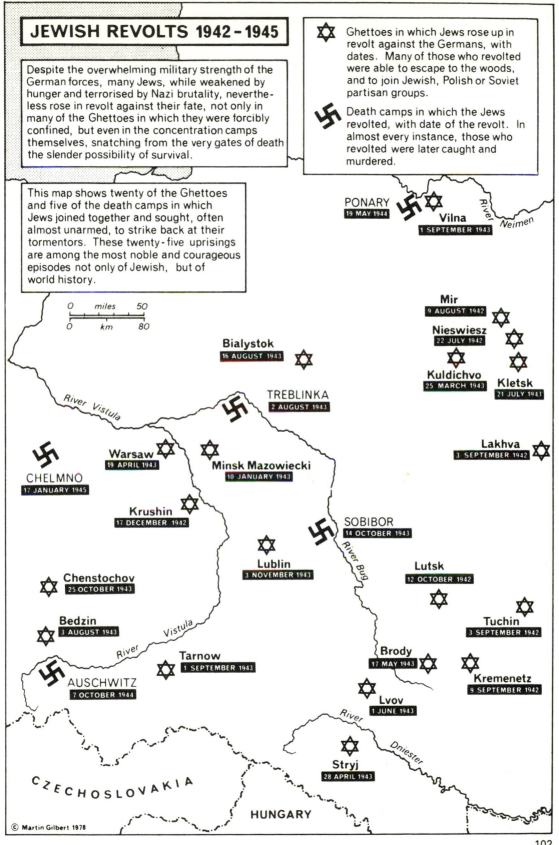

JEWISH REVOLTS 1942-1945

Despite the overwhelming military strength of the German forces, many Jews, while weakened by hunger and terrorised by Nazi brutality, nevertheless rose in revolt against their fate, not only in many of the Ghettoes in which they were forcibly confined, but even in the concentration camps themselves, snatching from the very gates of death the slender possibility of survival.

✡ Ghettoes in which Jews rose up in revolt against the Germans, with dates. Many of those who revolted were able to escape to the woods, and to join Jewish, Polish or Soviet partisan groups.

卍 Death camps in which the Jews revolted, with date of the revolt. In almost every instance, those who revolted were later caught and murdered.

This map shows twenty of the Ghettoes and five of the death camps in which Jews joined together and sought, often almost unarmed, to strike back at their tormentors. These twenty-five uprisings are among the most noble and courageous episodes not only of Jewish, but of world history.

PONARY
19 MAY 1944

Vilna
1 SEPTEMBER 1943

River Neimen

Mir
9 AUGUST 1942

Nieswiesz
22 JULY 1942

Kuldichvo
25 MARCH 1943

Kletsk
21 JULY 1943

0   miles   50
0   km   80

Bialystok
16 AUGUST 1943

TREBLINKA
2 AUGUST 1943

River Vistula

Warsaw
19 APRIL 1943

Minsk Mazowiecki
10 JANUARY 1943

Lakhva
3 SEPTEMBER 1942

CHELMNO
17 JANUARY 1945

Krushin
17 DECEMBER 1942

SOBIBOR
14 OCTOBER 1943

River Bug

Lublin
3 NOVEMBER 1943

Lutsk
12 OCTOBER 1942

Chenstochov
25 OCTOBER 1943

Tuchin
3 SEPTEMBER 1942

Bedzin
3 AUGUST 1943

Vistula

Tarnow
1 SEPTEMBER 1943

River Vistula

Brody
17 MAY 1943

Kremenetz
9 SEPTEMBER 1942

AUSCHWITZ
7 OCTOBER 1944

Lvov
1 JUNE 1943

River Dniester

Stryj
28 APRIL 1943

C Z E C H O S L O V A K I A

HUNGARY

© Martin Gilbert 1978

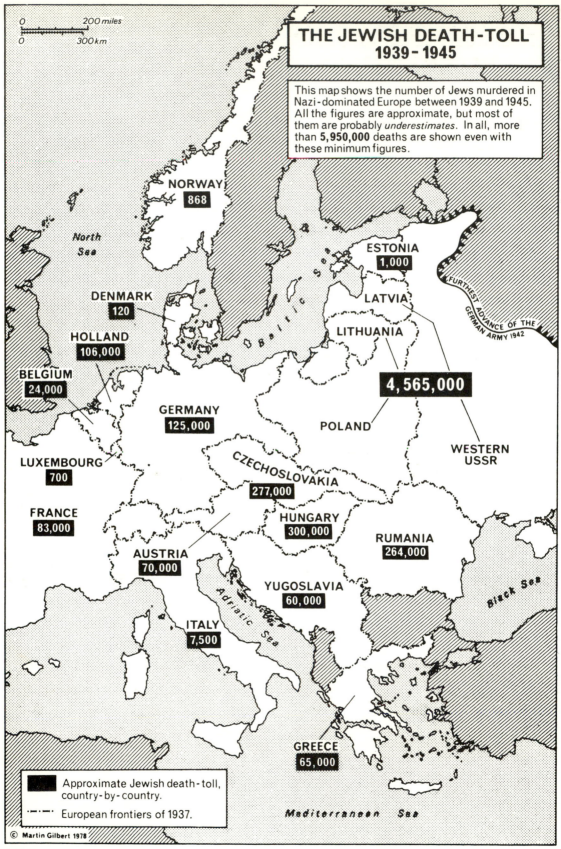

THE JEWISH DEATH-TOLL
1939-1945

This map shows the number of Jews murdered in Nazi-dominated Europe between 1939 and 1945. All the figures are approximate, but most of them are probably *underestimates*. In all, more than **5,950,000** deaths are shown even with these minimum figures.

0 — 200 miles
0 — 300 km

North Sea

NORWAY
868

ESTONIA
1,000

LATVIA

DENMARK
120

LITHUANIA

FURTHEST ADVANCE OF THE GERMAN ARMY 1942

HOLLAND
106,000

BELGIUM
24,000

4,565,000

GERMANY
125,000

POLAND

WESTERN USSR

LUXEMBOURG
700

CZECHOSLOVAKIA
277,000

FRANCE
83,000

HUNGARY
300,000

RUMANIA
264,000

AUSTRIA
70,000

YUGOSLAVIA
60,000

Black Sea

ITALY
7,500

Adriatic Sea

GREECE
65,000

■ Approximate Jewish death-toll, country-by-country.

— · — European frontiers of 1937.

© Martin Gilbert 1978

Mediterranean Sea

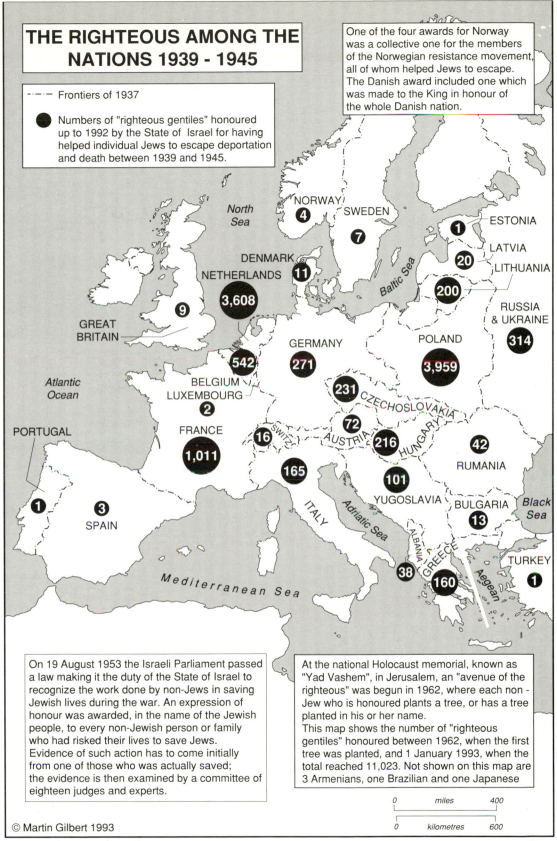

THE RIGHTEOUS AMONG THE NATIONS 1939 - 1945

One of the four awards for Norway was a collective one for the members of the Norwegian resistance movement, all of whom helped Jews to escape. The Danish award included one which was made to the King in honour of the whole Danish nation.

-·-·- Frontiers of 1937

● Numbers of "righteous gentiles" honoured up to 1992 by the State of Israel for having helped individual Jews to escape deportation and death between 1939 and 1945.

North Sea

NORWAY **4**

SWEDEN **7**

ESTONIA **1**

LATVIA **20**

LITHUANIA **200**

RUSSIA & UKRAINE **314**

Baltic Sea

DENMARK
NETHERLANDS **11**
3,608

GREAT BRITAIN **9**

GERMANY **271**

POLAND **3,959**

BELGIUM **542**
LUXEMBOURG **2**

231

CZECHOSLOVAKIA

72

AUSTRIA

HUNGARY **216**

RUMANIA **42**

Atlantic Ocean

PORTUGAL **1**

SPAIN **3**

FRANCE **1,011**

SWITZ. **16**

165

ITALY

101

YUGOSLAVIA

BULGARIA **13**

Black Sea

Adriatic Sea

ALBANIA **38**

GREECE **160**

Aegean

TURKEY **1**

M e d i t e r r a n e a n   S e a

On 19 August 1953 the Israeli Parliament passed a law making it the duty of the State of Israel to recognize the work done by non-Jews in saving Jewish lives during the war. An expression of honour was awarded, in the name of the Jewish people, to every non-Jewish person or family who had risked their lives to save Jews. Evidence of such action has to come initially from one of those who was actually saved; the evidence is then examined by a committee of eighteen judges and experts.

At the national Holocaust memorial, known as "Yad Vashem", in Jerusalem, an "avenue of the righteous" was begun in 1962, where each non-Jew who is honoured plants a tree, or has a tree planted in his or her name.
This map shows the number of "righteous gentiles" honoured between 1962, when the first tree was planted, and 1 January 1993, when the total reached 11,023. Not shown on this map are 3 Armenians, one Brazilian and one Japanese

| 0 | miles | 400 |
| 0 | kilometres | 600 |

© Martin Gilbert 1993

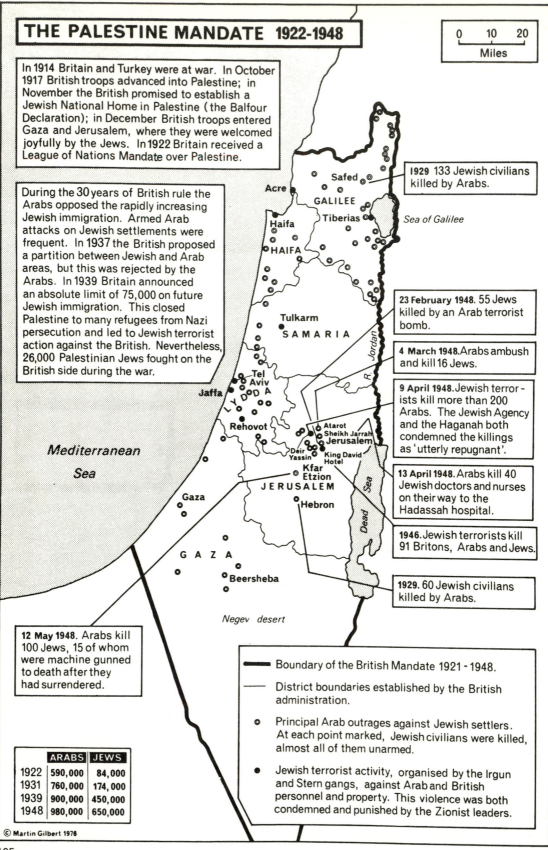

THE PALESTINE MANDATE 1922-1948

Scale: 0 10 20 Miles

In 1914 Britain and Turkey were at war. In October 1917 British troops advanced into Palestine; in November the British promised to establish a Jewish National Home in Palestine (the Balfour Declaration); in December British troops entered Gaza and Jerusalem, where they were welcomed joyfully by the Jews. In 1922 Britain received a League of Nations Mandate over Palestine.

During the 30 years of British rule the Arabs opposed the rapidly increasing Jewish immigration. Armed Arab attacks on Jewish settlements were frequent. In 1937 the British proposed a partition between Jewish and Arab areas, but this was rejected by the Arabs. In 1939 Britain announced an absolute limit of 75,000 on future Jewish immigration. This closed Palestine to many refugees from Nazi persecution and led to Jewish terrorist action against the British. Nevertheless, 26,000 Palestinian Jews fought on the British side during the war.

1929 133 Jewish civilians killed by Arabs.

23 February 1948. 55 Jews killed by an Arab terrorist bomb.

4 March 1948. Arabs ambush and kill 16 Jews.

9 April 1948. Jewish terrorists kill more than 200 Arabs. The Jewish Agency and the Haganah both condemned the killings as 'utterly repugnant'.

13 April 1948. Arabs kill 40 Jewish doctors and nurses on their way to the Hadassah hospital.

1946. Jewish terrorists kill 91 Britons, Arabs and Jews.

1929. 60 Jewish civilians killed by Arabs.

12 May 1948. Arabs kill 100 Jews, 15 of whom were machine gunned to death after they had surrendered.

Map labels: Safed, Acre, GALILEE, Tiberias, Sea of Galilee, Haifa, HAIFA, Tulkarm, SAMARIA, R. Jordan, Tel Aviv, Jaffa, LYDDA, Rehovot, Atarot, Sheikh Jarrah, Jerusalem, Deir Yassin, King David Hotel, Kfar Etzion, JERUSALEM, Hebron, Dead Sea, Gaza, GAZA, Beersheba, Mediterranean Sea, Negev desert

Legend:

— Boundary of the British Mandate 1921-1948.

— District boundaries established by the British administration.

⊙ Principal Arab outrages against Jewish settlers. At each point marked, Jewish civilians were killed, almost all of them unarmed.

● Jewish terrorist activity, organised by the Irgun and Stern gangs, against Arab and British personnel and property. This violence was both condemned and punished by the Zionist leaders.

	ARABS	JEWS
1922	590,000	84,000
1931	760,000	174,000
1939	900,000	450,000
1948	980,000	650,000

© Martin Gilbert 1976

JEWISH OWNED LAND IN PALESTINE BY 1942

"For though thy people Israel be as the sand of the sea, yet a remnant of them shall return"

ISAIAH 10, 22

Metulla

Hanita

Safad
Rosh Pinha

Acre

EMEK ZEBULON

Haifa

L. Tiberias

Nahalal

Tel Or

Zichron Jacob

Balfourya

Jenin

Hadera

Nathanya

Nablus

Herzlya

Petah Tikva

Tel Aviv
Jaffa

Rishon le Zion

Rehovot

Jerusalem

Bethlehem

Hebron

Gaza

Jordan

Dead Sea

Beersheba

British Mandate 1920-1948

Jewish owned land, April 1942

0   10
Miles

OTHER ZIONS 1652-1946

11 1884 First colony of Russian Jews, established by London Mansion House Committee. By 1902 several thousand Jews had settled in Saskatchewan

10 1880-1902 Russian and Rumanian Jews look to Cyprus as a Jewish national home. Several hundred Jews bought land

5 1819 Proposal for a Jewish colony along the upper Mississippi and Missouri rivers

4 c.1730 Hermann Moritz of Saxony argues in favour of a Jewish State in South America with himself as King

7 1825 Mordecai Noah establishes Jewish "State" of Ararat on Grand Island near Niagara Falls. Some Jews settled here in 1826

2 1654 British ruled (1650-1657) seen as a possible haven for the Jews of Europe

1 1652 Dutch West India Company establishes Jewish colony

15 1904 A thousand Jews establish a colony in Brazil

3 1659 French West India Company supports plans for a Jewish colony

13 1903 British Government offers El Arish to the Jews, but the British Agent in Egypt refuses to allow the colony to use water from the Nile for irrigation

12 1892 Baron de Hirsch sets up Jewish Colonization Association aimed at settling 3,000,000 Jews from Russia in Argentina. Only 45,000 settlers by 1914, after which numbers fell

14 1903 British offer Guas Ngishu plateau of Kenya to the Jews, but this was rejected in 1905 by Zionists, who demanded Palestine, then under Turkish rule

CANADA

UNITED STATES

Curacao

Surinam · Cayenne

BRAZIL
Recife

ARGENTINE

"O that I had wings like a dove!
For then I would fly away and be at rest"
PSALM 55

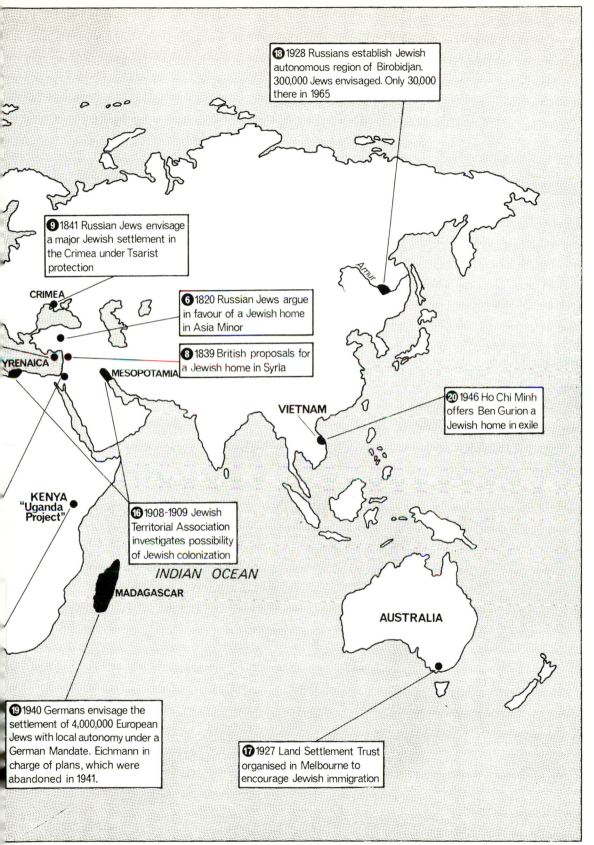

18 1928 Russians establish Jewish autonomous region of Birobidjan. 300,000 Jews envisaged. Only 30,000 there in 1965

9 1841 Russian Jews envisage a major Jewish settlement in the Crimea under Tsarist protection

CRIMEA

Amur

6 1820 Russian Jews argue in favour of a Jewish home in Asia Minor

8 1839 British proposals for a Jewish home in Syria

YRENAICA

MESOPOTAMIA

VIETNAM

20 1946 Ho Chi Minh offers Ben Gurion a Jewish home in exile

KENYA "Uganda Project"

16 1908-1909 Jewish Territorial Association investigates possibility of Jewish colonization

INDIAN OCEAN

MADAGASCAR

AUSTRALIA

19 1940 Germans envisage the settlement of 4,000,000 European Jews with local autonomy under a German Mandate. Eichmann in charge of plans, which were abandoned in 1941.

17 1927 Land Settlement Trust organised in Melbourne to encourage Jewish immigration

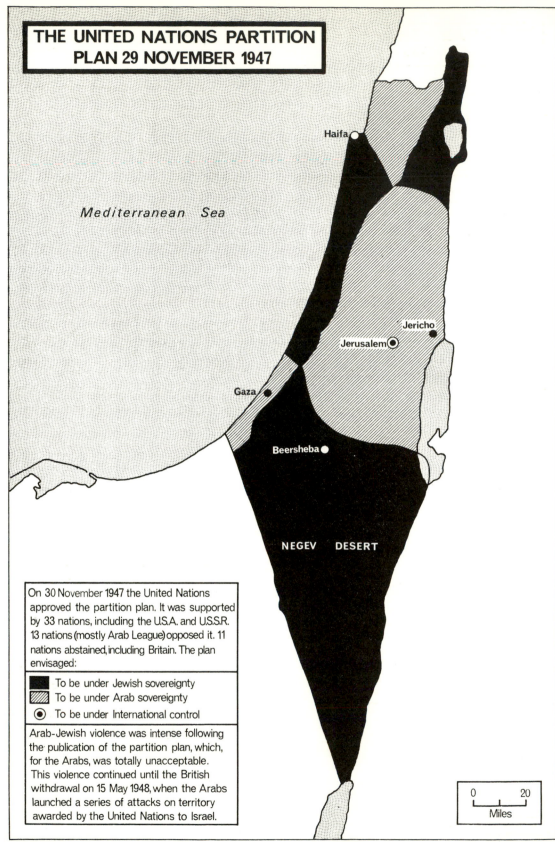

THE UNITED NATIONS PARTITION PLAN 29 NOVEMBER 1947

Mediterranean Sea

Haifa

Jericho

Jerusalem

Gaza

Beersheba

NEGEV DESERT

On 30 November 1947 the United Nations approved the partition plan. It was supported by 33 nations, including the U.S.A. and U.S.S.R. 13 nations (mostly Arab League) opposed it. 11 nations abstained, including Britain. The plan envisaged:

▇ To be under Jewish sovereignty
▨ To be under Arab sovereignty
◉ To be under International control

Arab-Jewish violence was intense following the publication of the partition plan, which, for the Arabs, was totally unacceptable. This violence continued until the British withdrawal on 15 May 1948, when the Arabs launched a series of attacks on territory awarded by the United Nations to Israel.

0   20
Miles

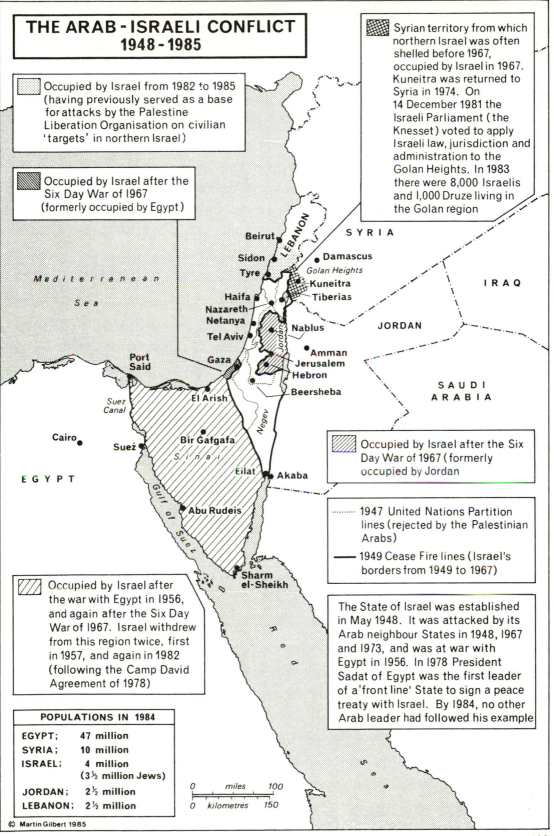

THE ARAB-ISRAELI CONFLICT
1948-1985

Occupied by Israel from 1982 to 1985 (having previously served as a base for attacks by the Palestine Liberation Organisation on civilian 'targets' in northern Israel)

Occupied by Israel after the Six Day War of 1967 (formerly occupied by Egypt)

Syrian territory from which northern Israel was often shelled before 1967, occupied by Israel in 1967. Kuneitra was returned to Syria in 1974. On 14 December 1981 the Israeli Parliament (the Knesset) voted to apply Israeli law, jurisdiction and administration to the Golan Heights. In 1983 there were 8,000 Israelis and 1,000 Druze living in the Golan region

Mediterranean Sea

Beirut

Sidon
Tyre

LEBANON

S Y R I A

Damascus

Golan Heights

Kuneitra
Tiberias

I R A Q

Haifa
Nazareth
Netanya

Tel Aviv

Nablus

JORDAN

Gaza

Port Said

El Arish

Suez Canal

Amman
Jerusalem
Hebron

Beersheba

S A U D I
A R A B I A

Cairo

Suez

Negev

Sinai

Bir Gafgafa

E G Y P T

Eilat   Akaba

Gulf of Suez

Abu Rudeis

Occupied by Israel after the Six Day War of 1967 (formerly occupied by Jordan

1947 United Nations Partition lines (rejected by the Palestinian Arabs)

1949 Cease Fire lines (Israel's borders from 1949 to 1967)

Sharm el-Sheikh

Occupied by Israel after the war with Egypt in 1956, and again after the Six Day War of 1967. Israel withdrew from this region twice, first in 1957, and again in 1982 (following the Camp David Agreement of 1978)

The State of Israel was established in May 1948. It was attacked by its Arab neighbour States in 1948, 1967 and 1973, and was at war with Egypt in 1956. In 1978 President Sadat of Egypt was the first leader of a 'front line' State to sign a peace treaty with Israel. By 1984, no other Arab leader had followed his example

R e d

S e a

POPULATIONS IN 1984	
EGYPT;	47 million
SYRIA;	10 million
ISRAEL;	4 million
	(3½ million Jews)
JORDAN;	2½ million
LEBANON;	2½ million

0   miles   100
0   kilometres   150

© Martin Gilbert 1985

THE RETURN OF JEWS TO ZION 1948-1964

SWEDEN
400

BELGIUM
1,000

HOLLAND
1,000

BRITAIN

2,000

GERMANY

POLAND

104,

CZECHOSLOVAKIA

40,000

FRANCE

SWITZERLAND

AUSTRIA

HUNGARY

RUMAN

400

9,000

3,000

14,000

YUGOSLAVIA

SPAIN

4,000

ITALY

BULGAR

400

1,500

8,000

GREECE

MOROCCO

ALGERIA

3,500

TUNISIA

120,000

30,000

LIBYA

35,000

Jewish population of Israel	
1948	657,000
1950	1,203,000
1958	1,810,000
1962	2,069,000

Over 50,000 Jews returning to Israel

Over 10,000 Jews returning to Israel

Over 1,000 Jews returning to Israel

"I will even gather you from the people, and assemble you out of the countries where ye have been scattered, and I will give you the land of Israel"

EZEKIEL 11,17

TURKEY

SYRIA

IRAQ

IRAN

AFGHANISTAN

37,000

26,000

123,000

139,000

3,880

75,000

Operation "MAGIC CARPET"

48,000

6,500

YEMEN

ADEN

0   200
Miles

JERUSALEM: DIVIDED CITY 1948-1967

From 1949 to 1966 Jordan refused access to Israeli's wishing to visit Old Jerusalem. In June 1967 Israel occupied the Old City, destroyed the partition barriers, and established an Israeli administration for the whole city

War Cemetery

Mount

Scopus

Hadassah Medical Centre

ISRAEL

Hebrew University and National Library

SHEIKH JARRAH

AMERICAN COLONY

MAHANAYIM

GEULA

Mandelbaum Gate

Strauss Health Centre

Hospital

Tombs of the Kings

St George's Cathedral

Herods Gate

Rockefeller Museum

Hadassah Headquarters

MUSLIM QUARTER

St. Stephen's Gate

Mount of Olives

Gethsemane

Bezalel Museum

CHRISTIAN QUARTER

New Gate

The Holy Sepulchre

MORIA

Wailing Wall

Dome of the Rock

Ratisbon Monastery

Yeshurun Synagogue

David's Tower

El Aksa Mosque

Absalom's Tomb

ISRAEL

ARMENIAN QUARTER

Hurva Synagogue

REHAVIA

JEWISH QUARTER

Dung Gate

JORDAN

Greek Monastery

King David's Tomb

Mount Zion

TALBIYEH

GERMAN COLONY

Railway Station

EL QATAMON

GREEK COLONY

BAQAA

TALPIOTH

JORDAN

▬▬▬	Western armistice-line
———	Eastern armistice-line
▓▓	No Man's Land
╱╱	Built-up areas
▬ ▬	Important buildings
+++	Railway
∿∿∿	Wall of the Old City

0   500
Yards

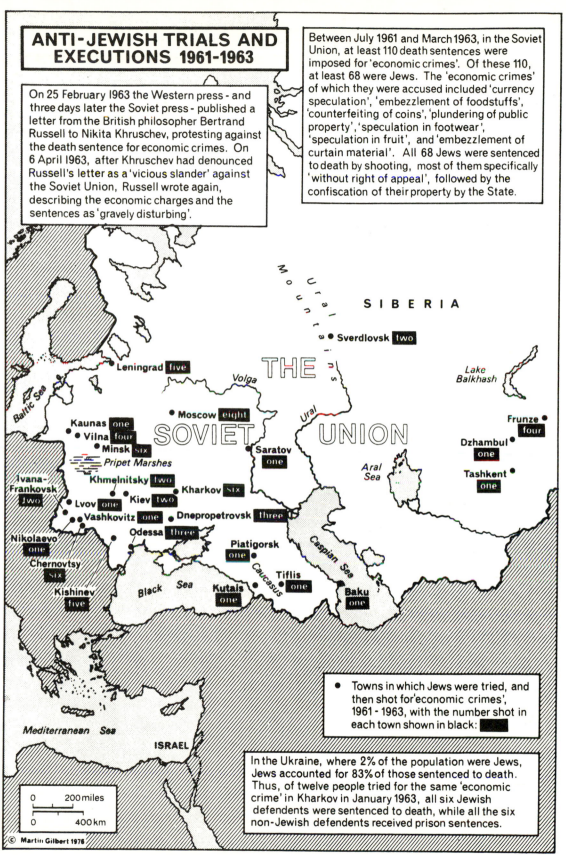

ANTI-JEWISH TRIALS AND EXECUTIONS 1961-1963

On 25 February 1963 the Western press - and three days later the Soviet press - published a letter from the British philosopher Bertrand Russell to Nikita Khruschev, protesting against the death sentence for economic crimes. On 6 April 1963, after Khruschev had denounced Russell's letter as a 'vicious slander' against the Soviet Union, Russell wrote again, describing the economic charges and the sentences as 'gravely disturbing'.

Between July 1961 and March 1963, in the Soviet Union, at least 110 death sentences were imposed for 'economic crimes'. Of these 110, at least 68 were Jews. The 'economic crimes' of which they were accused included 'currency speculation', 'embezzlement of foodstuffs', 'counterfeiting of coins', 'plundering of public property', 'speculation in footwear', 'speculation in fruit', and 'embezzlement of curtain material'. All 68 Jews were sentenced to death by shooting, most of them specifically 'without right of appeal', followed by the confiscation of their property by the State.

S I B E R I A

Ural Mountains

THE

SOVIET UNION

Sverdlovsk `two`

Lake Balkhash

Leningrad `five`

Volga

Ural

Moscow `eight`

Frunze `four`

Kaunas `one`
Vilna `four`
Minsk `six`

Saratov `one`

Dzhambul `one`

Pripet Marshes

Aral Sea

Tashkent `one`

Khmelnitsky `two`

Kharkov `six`

Ivana-Frankovsk `two`

Lvov `one` Kiev `two`

Vashkovitz `one`   Dnepropetrovsk `three`

Nikolaevo `one`

Odessa `three`

Piatigorsk `one`

Caspian Sea

Chernovtsy `six`

Kishinev `five`

Black   Sea

Kutais `one`

Caucasus

Tiflis `one`

Baku `one`

Baltic Sea

Mediterranean Sea

ISRAEL

● Towns in which Jews were tried, and then shot for 'economic crimes', 1961 - 1963, with the number shot in each town shown in black: ▓▓▓

In the Ukraine, where 2% of the population were Jews, Jews accounted for 83% of those sentenced to death. Thus, of twelve people tried for the same 'economic crime' in Kharkov in January 1963, all six Jewish defendants were sentenced to death, while all the six non-Jewish defendants received prison sentences.

0   200 miles
0   400 km

© Martin Gilbert 1976

THE JEWS OF IRAQ IN THE TWENTIETH CENTURY

0 — 50 Miles

1935 Jews removed from Government Service. Many Jews forbidden to travel to Palestine
1936 Ten Jews killed by Arab riots in Baghdad and Basra. Teaching of Hebrew prohibited
1947 No Jewish children accepted in Government schools
August 1948 Zionism declared a crime (with Nazism, Communism, Atheism and Anarchism) Many Jews imprisoned, some hanged
10 March 1950 Official decree confiscates all property of Jews leaving for Israel, and appoints a special custodian to sell it by public auction. All emigrants' bank accounts seized by the State
25 February 1958 Abolition of Jewish Community Status. All community property, including schools and hospitals, transferred to Government

3 March 1968 Law № 10 forbids Jews to receive more than 100 Iraqi dinars per month for sale of immovable property (in 1948 the Jewish community had been made to pay 250,000 dinars towards the Iraqi war effort against Israel, and towards the Palestinian Arab refugees)
1969 Nine Jews hanged for 'Zionist' activities in January; 2 hanged for 'spying for Israel and the CIA' in August; 2 killed in September; 4 killed in November
October 1972 Many Jews arrested. 16 disappear without trace. More than 20 murdered
April 1973 A family of 5 Jews murdered in their home

JEWISH POPULATION	
1948	135,000
1971	2,500
1974	400

1933 20 Jews murdered

Dec 1947 A Jew accused of trying to inject cholera germs in water drunk by Arab children

October 1948 President of the local Jewish Community arrested on charge of maintaining contact with his sons in Israel

May 1947 Following destruction of much Jewish property by mob attack, Jews forced to move to Baghdad

⊙ Towns with Jewish communities in 1947

July 1937 Violent anti-Jewish demonstrations. Jewish property destroyed
June 1941 During riots following collapse of pro-Nazi Government of Rashid Ali, 175 Jews killed and 1,000 injured. Much looting of Jewish property. 900 Jewish houses destroyed. Many Jews tortured
July 1946 Anti-Jewish riots. Hundreds of Jews wounded and much property destroyed
May 1947 A Jew murdered by a mob which accused him of giving poisoned sweets to an Arab child
Dec 1949 Anti-Jewish riots, many injured

September–October 1948 Many wealthy Jews arrested. One, a millionaire, hanged and his fortune seized. His cousin died after four months in prison. All were accused of allegedly supplying arms to the 'Zionists'

Place names on map: Amadiya, Rowanduz, Zakho, Fishkhabur, Aqra, Dehok, Harir, Mosul, Arbil, Rania, Kirkuk, Tuz Khurmato, Sulaimaniya, Halabcha, Kifri, Kara-Tepe, Khanaqin, Muqdadiyah, Khalis, Ana, Euphrates River, Ramadi, Faluja, Bakuba, Baghdad, Mandali, Musaiyib, Hindiya, Hilla, Kut-al-Hayy, Kut, Diwaniya, Shamiya, Amara, Kalat Salih, Nasiriya, Samawa, Uzair, Basra, Tigris River, SYRIA, IRAQ, JORDAN, SAUDI ARABIA, IRAN, KUWAIT, Persian Gulf

SAMPLE ORIGINS OF ISRAELI JEWRY 1960

0 — 300
Miles

GERMANY
5

POLAND

RUSSIA
52

AUSTRIA-HUNGARY
3

3
RUMANIA

BULGARIA
1

ISRAEL
9

The birthplace of the 73 Members of the Fourth Knesset whose birthplace is given in "Who's Who Israel 1960"

SAMPLE ORIGINS OF UNITED STATES JEWRY 1965

RUSSIA
41

GERMANY
6

POLAND

U.S.A.
55

AUSTRIA-HUNGARY
7

3
RUMANIA

1

T U R K E Y

The birthplace of the 114 distinguished Americans who died in 1965 and whose birthplace is given in the American Jewish Yearbook for 1966

PALESTINE
1

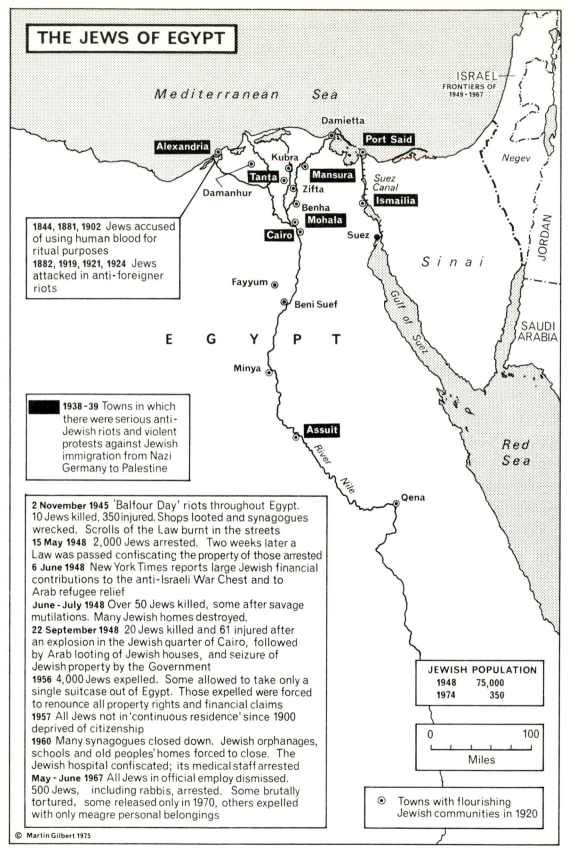

THE JEWS OF EGYPT

Mediterranean Sea

ISRAEL
FRONTIERS OF
1949-1967

Negev

Damietta

Alexandria

Kubra

Port Said

Tanta

Mansura

Suez Canal

Zifta

Damanhur

Ismailia

Benha

Mohala

Cairo

Suez

Sinai

JORDAN

1844, 1881, 1902 Jews accused
of using human blood for
ritual purposes
1882, 1919, 1921, 1924 Jews
attacked in anti-foreigner
riots

Fayyum

Beni Suef

SAUDI
ARABIA

E   G   Y   P   T

Minya

Gulf of Suez

1938-39 Towns in which
there were serious anti-
Jewish riots and violent
protests against Jewish
immigration from Nazi
Germany to Palestine

Assuit

River Nile

Red Sea

2 November 1945 'Balfour Day' riots throughout Egypt.
10 Jews killed, 350 injured. Shops looted and synagogues
wrecked. Scrolls of the Law burnt in the streets
15 May 1948 2,000 Jews arrested. Two weeks later a
Law was passed confiscating the property of those arrested
6 June 1948 New York Times reports large Jewish financial
contributions to the anti-Israeli War Chest and to
Arab refugee relief
June - July 1948 Over 50 Jews killed, some after savage
mutilations. Many Jewish homes destroyed.
22 September 1948 20 Jews killed and 61 injured after
an explosion in the Jewish quarter of Cairo, followed
by Arab looting of Jewish houses, and seizure of
Jewish property by the Government
1956 4,000 Jews expelled. Some allowed to take only a
single suitcase out of Egypt. Those expelled were forced
to renounce all property rights and financial claims
1957 All Jews not in 'continuous residence' since 1900
deprived of citizenship
1960 Many synagogues closed down. Jewish orphanages,
schools and old peoples' homes forced to close. The
Jewish hospital confiscated; its medical staff arrested
May - June 1967 All Jews in official employ dismissed.
500 Jews, including rabbis, arrested. Some brutally
tortured, some released only in 1970, others expelled
with only meagre personal belongings

Qena

JEWISH POPULATION	
1948	75,000
1974	350

0	100
Miles	

⊙ Towns with flourishing
    Jewish communities in 1920

© Martin Gilbert 1975

116

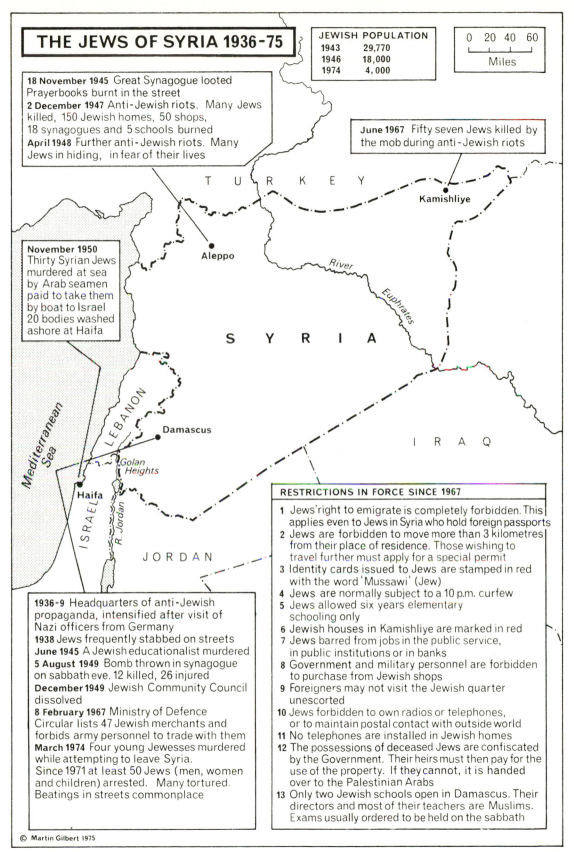

THE JEWS OF SYRIA 1936-75

JEWISH POPULATION	
1943	29,770
1946	18,000
1974	4,000

0 20 40 60
Miles

18 November 1945 Great Synagogue looted Prayerbooks burnt in the street
2 December 1947 Anti-Jewish riots. Many Jews killed, 150 Jewish homes, 50 shops, 18 synagogues and 5 schools burned
April 1948 Further anti-Jewish riots. Many Jews in hiding, in fear of their lives

June 1967 Fifty seven Jews killed by the mob during anti-Jewish riots

November 1950 Thirty Syrian Jews murdered at sea by Arab seamen paid to take them by boat to Israel 20 bodies washed ashore at Haifa

T U R K E Y

Kamishliye

Aleppo

River Euphrates

S Y R I A

Mediterranean Sea

LEBANON

Damascus

Golan Heights

Haifa

ISRAEL

R. Jordan

JORDAN

I R A Q

1936-9 Headquarters of anti-Jewish propaganda, intensified after visit of Nazi officers from Germany
1938 Jews frequently stabbed on streets
June 1945 A Jewish educationalist murdered
5 August 1949 Bomb thrown in synagogue on sabbath eve. 12 killed, 26 injured
December 1949 Jewish Community Council dissolved
8 February 1967 Ministry of Defence Circular lists 47 Jewish merchants and forbids army personnel to trade with them
March 1974 Four young Jewesses murdered while attempting to leave Syria.
Since 1971 at least 50 Jews (men, women and children) arrested. Many tortured. Beatings in streets commonplace

RESTRICTIONS IN FORCE SINCE 1967

1 Jews' right to emigrate is completely forbidden. This applies even to Jews in Syria who hold foreign passports
2 Jews are forbidden to move more than 3 kilometres from their place of residence. Those wishing to travel further must apply for a special permit
3 Identity cards issued to Jews are stamped in red with the word 'Mussawi' (Jew)
4 Jews are normally subject to a 10 p.m. curfew
5 Jews allowed six years elementary schooling only
6 Jewish houses in Kamishliye are marked in red
7 Jews barred from jobs in the public service, in public institutions or in banks
8 Government and military personnel are forbidden to purchase from Jewish shops
9 Foreigners may not visit the Jewish quarter unescorted
10 Jews forbidden to own radios or telephones, or to maintain postal contact with outside world
11 No telephones are installed in Jewish homes
12 The possessions of deceased Jews are confiscated by the Government. Their heirs must then pay for the use of the property. If they cannot, it is handed over to the Palestinian Arabs
13 Only two Jewish schools open in Damascus. Their directors and most of their teachers are Muslims. Exams usually ordered to be held on the sabbath

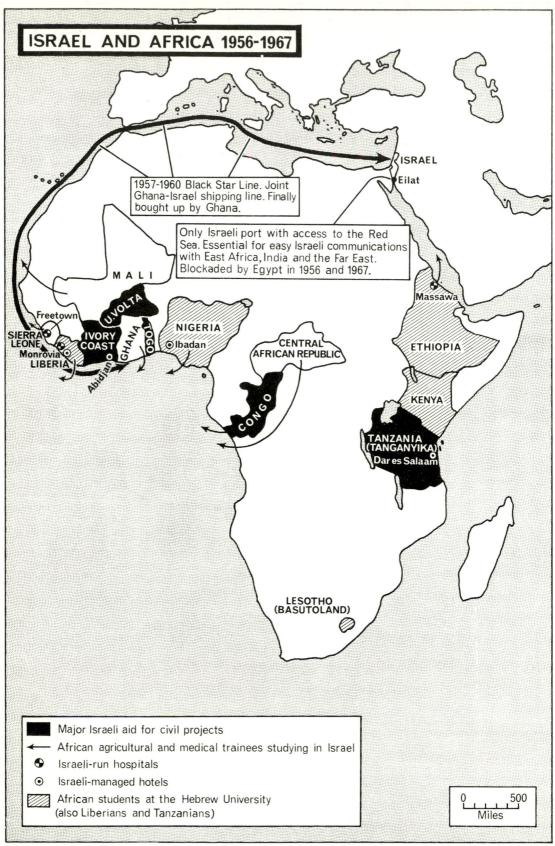

ISRAEL AND AFRICA 1956-1967

1957-1960 Black Star Line. Joint Ghana-Israel shipping line. Finally bought up by Ghana.

Only Israeli port with access to the Red Sea. Essential for easy Israeli communications with East Africa, India and the Far East. Blockaded by Egypt in 1956 and 1967.

ISRAEL

Eilat

Massawa

MALI

U.VOLTA

Freetown

SIERRA LEONE

GHANA

TOGO

IVORY COAST

Abidjan

Monrovia

LIBERIA

NIGERIA

Ibadan

CENTRAL AFRICAN REPUBLIC

ETHIOPIA

KENYA

CONGO

TANZANIA (TANGANYIKA)

Dar es Salaam

LESOTHO (BASUTOLAND)

◼ Major Israeli aid for civil projects

← African agricultural and medical trainees studying in Israel

◉ Israeli-run hospitals

⊙ Israeli-managed hotels

▨ African students at the Hebrew University (also Liberians and Tanzanians)

0   500
Miles

EXODUS FROM ETHIOPIA, 1974-1984

The Black Jews of Ethiopia, known as the Falashas ('Strangers'), were living in Ethiopia 2,000 years ago, possibly the descendents of Jewish settlers from southern Arabia, or of Jewish mercenaries settled on Elephantine Island to defend Egypt against Nubia in 659 BC, when they revolted and fled southward. After widespread conversions to Christianity in the 4th century, those still faithful to Judaism were persecuted, and fled into the mountains north of Lake Tana. Many wars were fought against them, one Ethiopian ruler giving himself the title 'Exterminator of the Jews'.

In 1905 the Polish-born Jacques Faitlovitch, having visited Ethiopia, argued that the Falashas were Jews, and needed Jewish help against Christian missionary activity. In 1923 he opened a boarding school in Addis Ababa for Falasha children. Settling in Israel in 1948, he argued that the Falashas were 'the descendents of genuine Jews and an integral part of the Jewish people'.

In 1974 there were more than 25,000 Black Jews in Ethiopia: 200 had already made their way to Israel, where the Sephardi Chief Rabbi had ruled, in 1972, that they were Jews. In 1975 an Israeli Cabinet Committee ruled that the Law of Return (the right of any Jew to go to Israel and become a citizen) applied to the Falashas.

In 1977 Israel's Prime Minister, Menachem Begin, encouraged Government action to bring Ethiopian Jews to Israel on a large scale. By 1984, there was 7,000 Ethiopian Jews in Israel. In 1984 and 1985 the Israeli Government carried out 'Operation Moses', to bring a further 10,000 Ethiopian Jews to Israel, by means of a massive airlift, from a region beset by civil war and famine.

© Martin Gilbert 1985

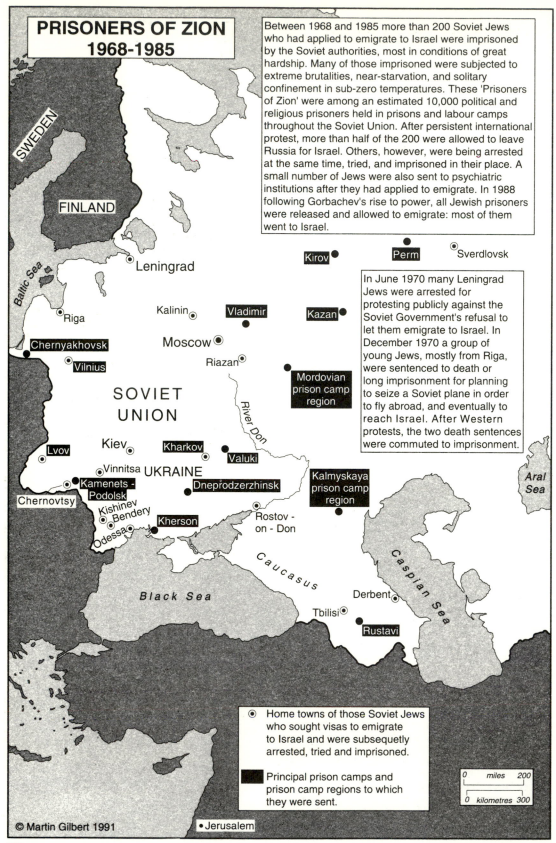

PRISONERS OF ZION
1968-1985

Between 1968 and 1985 more than 200 Soviet Jews who had applied to emigrate to Israel were imprisoned by the Soviet authorities, most in conditions of great hardship. Many of those imprisoned were subjected to extreme brutalities, near-starvation, and solitary confinement in sub-zero temperatures. These 'Prisoners of Zion' were among an estimated 10,000 political and religious prisoners held in prisons and labour camps throughout the Soviet Union. After persistent international protest, more than half of the 200 were allowed to leave Russia for Israel. Others, however, were being arrested at the same time, tried, and imprisoned in their place. A small number of Jews were also sent to psychiatric institutions after they had applied to emigrate. In 1988 following Gorbachev's rise to power, all Jewish prisoners were released and allowed to emigrate: most of them went to Israel.

In June 1970 many Leningrad Jews were arrested for protesting publicly against the Soviet Government's refusal to let them emigrate to Israel. In December 1970 a group of young Jews, mostly from Riga, were sentenced to death or long imprisonment for planning to seize a Soviet plane in order to fly abroad, and eventually to reach Israel. After Western protests, the two death sentences were commuted to imprisonment.

SWEDEN

FINLAND

Baltic Sea

Leningrad

Kirov

Perm

Sverdlovsk

Riga

Kalinin

Vladimir

Kazan

Chernyakhovsk

Vilnius

Moscow

Riazan

SOVIET UNION

River Don

Mordovian prison camp region

Lvov

Kiev

Kharkov

Valuki

Vinnitsa

UKRAINE

Kalmyskaya prison camp region

Aral Sea

Kamenets - Podolsk

Chernovtsy

Dneprodzerzhinsk

Kishinev

Bendery

Kherson

Rostov - on - Don

Odessa

Caucasus

Caspian Sea

Black Sea

Derbent

Tbilisi

Rustavi

⊙ Home towns of those Soviet Jews who sought visas to emigrate to Israel and were subsequetly arrested, tried and imprisoned.

■ Principal prison camps and prison camp regions to which they were sent.

0   miles   200

0   kilometres   300

© Martin Gilbert 1991

• Jerusalem

120

THE JEWS OF ALBANIA, 1945-1991

Pristina ●

Jews lived in Albania during Turkish rule (1478-1913) and during Albanian independence (1913-39). The community was granted official recognition on 2 April 1937. Under Italian rule (1939-43) local Jews were unharmed, but Jewish refugees from Yugoslavia were deported to Belgrade and killed. Under German rule (1943-44), 300 Albanian Jews were imprisoned in Pristina and 400 deported to Bergen-Belsen, of whom only 100 survived. In 1945 there were approximately 400 Jews in Albania.

Jews leaving for Israel (1990-1)	317
Jews leaving for the USA	37
Jews leaving for Greece	24
Jews remaining in Albania	57

YUGOSLAVIA

YUGOSLAVIA

Lake Skadar

Shkoder
15

Lezhe
9

Kruje
4

● Tirana
208

Durres
4

Kavaje
12

Lushnje
4

Fier
16

Lake Ohrid

Lake Prespan

Lake Mikri

Adriatic Sea

● Vlore
160

GREECE

Gjirokaster
3

Of Albania's 435 Jews in November 1990, 378 emigrated between then and May 1991, following the collapse of Communist control and the ending of emigration restrictions which had essentially held the Jewish community captive since 1945

CORFU

| 0 | miles | 30 |
| 0 | kilometres | 40 |

Martin Gilbert 1991

121

EMIGRATION FROM THE SOVIET UNION, ETHIOPIA AND ALBANIA 1989-1991

North Sea

Baltic Sea

Riga

Vilnius

Moscow

SOVIET UNION
330,000

Warsaw

Kiev

Kharkov

Vienna

Odessa

Budapest

Bucharest

Black Sea

Adriatic

Tirana

ALBANIA
317

Mediterranean Sea

The years 1989 to 1991 saw three remarkable waves of immigration to Israel. The first was the arrival of more than 330,000 Jews from the Soviet Union between October 1989 and December 1991 (a process still continuing). The second wave was 'Operation Solomon', the airlift in a single day of 14,200 Ethiopian Jews, the continuation and culmination of 'Operation Moses' (10,000 in 1984-5). The third wave was the arrival in Israel between November 1990 and April 1991 of 317 Jews of Albania, almost all of a community that had been totally cut off from the outside world since the imposition of Communist rule in 1945

ISRAEL

Among the 330,000 Jews reaching Israel from Russia were 8,000 doctors

Under Operations Moses (1984-5) and Solomon (1991) a total of 25,000 Ethiopian Jews were brought to Israel, leaving only 2,000 still in Ethiopia, all of whom were expected to reach Israel in 1991, thus ending one of the longest continuous settlements of Jews anywhere in the world (2,000 years)

In addition to the 330,000 Jews reaching Israel from Russia, a further 120,000 Soviet Jews emigrated to the United States between 1989 and 1991

Red Sea

TIGRE

Gondar

Addis Ababa

ETHIOPIA
14,200

0 — miles — 600

0 — kilometres — 800

© Martin Gilbert 1991

THE JEWISH WORLD IN 1991

PORTUGAL 300
RUMANIA 23,000
SPAIN 12,000
SWITZERLAND 18,300
SYRIA 4,000

HOLLAND 25,000
HUNGARY 90,000
ITALY 35,000
YUGOSLAVIA 5,500

DENMARK 9,000
GERMANY (W) 28,000
GERMANY (E) 400
GREECE 4,875

AUSTRIA 12,000
BELGIUM 30,000
BULGARIA 5,000
CZECHOSLOVAKIA 12,000

NORWAY 950 FINLAND 1,200
SWEDEN 16,000
DENMARK 9,000

JAPAN 600

HONG KONG 700

AUSTRALIA 90,000

NEW ZEALAND 4,800

CHINA 5

U.S.S.R 1,800,000

INDIA 6,000

IRAN 25,000

TURKEY 23,000

ISRAEL 4,100,000

SOUTH YEMEN 1,000

ETHIOPIA 1,000

ZIMBABWE 1,200

POLAND 6,000

TUNISIA 3,500

KENYA 330

ALGERIA 600

ZAMBIA 85

SOUTH AFRICA 120,000

GREAT BRITAIN 300,000

EIRE 2,000

FRANCE 535,000

MOROCCO 13,000

VENEZUELA 20,000

BOLIVIA 600

PARAGUAY 900

URUGUAY 44,000

ARGENTINA 228,000

COLOMBIA 7,000

CUBA 1,000

BRAZIL 150,000

CANADA 330,000

UNITED STATES 5,835,000

GUATEMALA 800

PANAMA 3,800

EQUADOR 1,000

PERU 5,000

CHILE 17,000

MEXICO 35,000

In 1991 there were an estimated 13,973,445 Jews in the world, of whom the three largest groups were in the United States, Israel and the Soviet Union respectively

Jewish populations in 1991

Main areas from which Jews have returned to Israel (Jewish population 4,100,000 in 1991) between 1948 and 1991, including 500,000 from the Soviet Union (1971-91)

© Martin Gilbert 1991

123

ANTI-SEMITIC INCIDENTS IN EUROPE, 1991

With the collapse of the East-West divide, and the end of the ideological confrontations of the Cold War, old forms of anti-Jewish feeling emerged throughout Europe, even in countries where the Jewish population was a fragment of what it had been before the Nazi destruction fifty years earlier. The anti-Jewish incidents shown on this map, and the responses to them, were reported by two leading news agencies, Reuters and Associated Press.

8 July anti-semitic posters displayed

Leningrad

Moscow

21 August During the attempted Communist coup, a Jew, Ilya Krichevsky, was one of the three people killed while protecting the Russian Parliament building. At the public funeral of the victims, Jewish prayers were recited

27 September More than fifty publications preach hatred of the Jews

5 October Mikhail Gorbachev declares: "The poisonous seeds of anti-Semitism even arose on Soviet soil"

6 October Boris Yeltsin issues a decree against anti-semitic activities

Black Sea

0 kilometres 250
0 miles 150

ESTONIA

LATVIA

LITHUANIA

Baltic Sea

6 August President Lech Walesa condemns the desecration of Jewish graves by vandals

Warsaw
POLAND

3 July At a memorial meeting to Jewish victims of Rumanian wartime fascism, Rumanian leaders speak out against anti-semitism in Rumania

Jassy

RUMANIA

Ravensbrück

EAST GERMANY

Dresden

6 November monument to Jewish victims of Nazi persecution desecrated

20 April Neo-Nazi march on the 102nd anniversary of Hitler's birth

Vienna

AUSTRIA

25 July a United States Senate Resolution condemns the resurgence of anti-semitism in Rumania

Adriatic Sea

9 October Graves broken open in the Jewish cemetery

24 October In an opinion poll, nearly one-third of Austrians admit to dislike of Jews

North Sea

© Martin Gilbert 1993

124

WORLDWIDE IMMIGRATION TO ISRAEL, 1992

COMMONWEALTH OF INDEPENDENT STATES
65,075

HUNGARY 134
RUMANIA 466
BULGARIA 306

INDIA
143

YEMEN
120

ETHIOPIA
3,568

SOUTH AFRICA
253

AUSTRALIA
122

NETHERLANDS 62

BELGIUM 85

GREAT BRITAIN 388

FRANCE 1,134

ISRAEL

Indian Ocean

Atlantic Ocean

Pacific Ocean

CANADA 209

UNITED STATES 1,676

MEXICO 31

COLOMBIA 17

BRAZIL 170

URUGUAY 47

ARGENTINA 312

CHILE 58

Of Israel's total Jewish population in 1992 (just over 4 million), 17% had been born in the Soviet Union

PRINCIPAL WAVES OF EMIGRATION FROM RUSSIA	
1951-1970	16,000
1971-1981	256,000
1982-1985	6,000
1986-1992	410,000
total	688,000

```
kilometres
0          3,000
0      miles  2,000
```

In 1992 a total of 76,554 Jews emigrated to Israel. This map shows their main countries of origin and their numbers. Jews from the Commonwealth of Independent States made up 84% of all immigrants

■ Countries from which Jews emigrated to Israel during 1992, with the number from each country

© Martin Gilbert 1993

THE JEWS OF THE FORMER SOVIET UNION, 1989 - 1993

Between the opening of the gates of emigration in 1989 and the end of 1992, more than 341,815 (21%) out of 1,640,600 Jews left the Soviet Union for Israel. This map shows the numbers living in each of the Republics of the Commonwealth of Independent States (established 21 December 1991), and the number (white on black) that left for Israel since 1 January 1989. A further 100,000 (7%) left for the United States and 60,000 (4%) to Germany

← direct flights, beginning 5 November 1991 from Moscow

ESTONIA
5,000
869 17%

LATVIA
22,000
5,045 23%

LITHUANIA
12,000
4,490 37%

BELARUS
110,000
41,444 38%

UKRAINE
550,000
107,277 20%

MOLDOVA
51,000
32,040 63%

RUSSIA
700,000
85,411 12%

GEORGIA
24,000
3,257 14%

AZERBAIJAN
30,000
14,280 48%

KAZAKHSTAN
28,000
3,937 14%

ARMENIA
600
406 48%

UZBEKISTAN
86,000
34,975 40%

3,000
263 9%

KYRGYZSTAN
6,000
1,922 32%

TAJIKISTAN
13,000
6,199 48%

North Sea

Baltic Sea

Vilnius

Riga

St Petersburg

Minsk

Moscow

River Volga

Kiev

Kishinev

Odessa

Black Sea

Sukhumi

Tbilisi

Baku

Caspian Sea

Aral Sea

TURKMENISTAN

Tashkent

Dushanbe

Mediterranean Sea

Tel Aviv

ISRAEL

The percentages of Jews leaving the Republics of the Commonwealth of Independent States varied from 9% to 68%. The largest number of emigrants were from those Republics in which civil strife and internal unrest was most wide-spread. By 1 January 1993, immigrants from the Soviet Union/Commonwealth of Independent States since 1951 made up the largest single immigrant group in Israel (surpassing the numbers of Jews born in Arab lands)

0 miles 500
0 kilometres 800

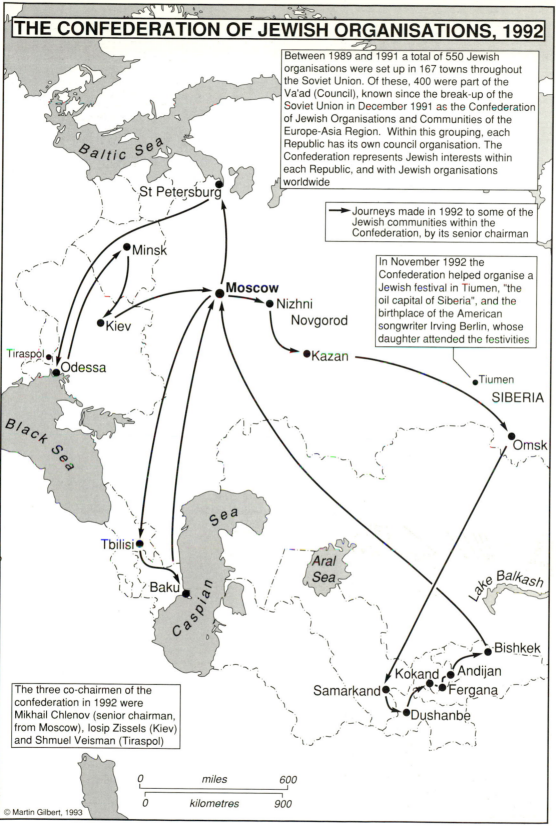

THE CONFEDERATION OF JEWISH ORGANISATIONS, 1992

Between 1989 and 1991 a total of 550 Jewish organisations were set up in 167 towns throughout the Soviet Union. Of these, 400 were part of the Va'ad (Council), known since the break-up of the Soviet Union in December 1991 as the Confederation of Jewish Organisations and Communities of the Europe-Asia Region. Within this grouping, each Republic has its own council organisation. The Confederation represents Jewish interests within each Republic, and with Jewish organisations worldwide

→ Journeys made in 1992 to some of the Jewish communities within the Confederation, by its senior chairman

In November 1992 the Confederation helped organise a Jewish festival in Tiumen, "the oil capital of Siberia", and the birthplace of the American songwriter Irving Berlin, whose daughter attended the festivities

The three co-chairmen of the confederation in 1992 were Mikhail Chlenov (senior chairman, from Moscow), Iosip Zissels (Kiev) and Shmuel Veisman (Tiraspol)

Baltic Sea

St Petersburg

Minsk

Moscow

Nizhni Novgorod

Kiev

Kazan

Tiraspol

Odessa

Tiumen

SIBERIA

Black Sea

Omsk

Caspian Sea

Aral Sea

Lake Balkash

Tbilisi

Baku

Bishkek

Kokand   Andijan

Samarkand   Fergana

Dushanbe

| 0 | miles | 600 |
| 0 | kilometres | 900 |

© Martin Gilbert, 1993

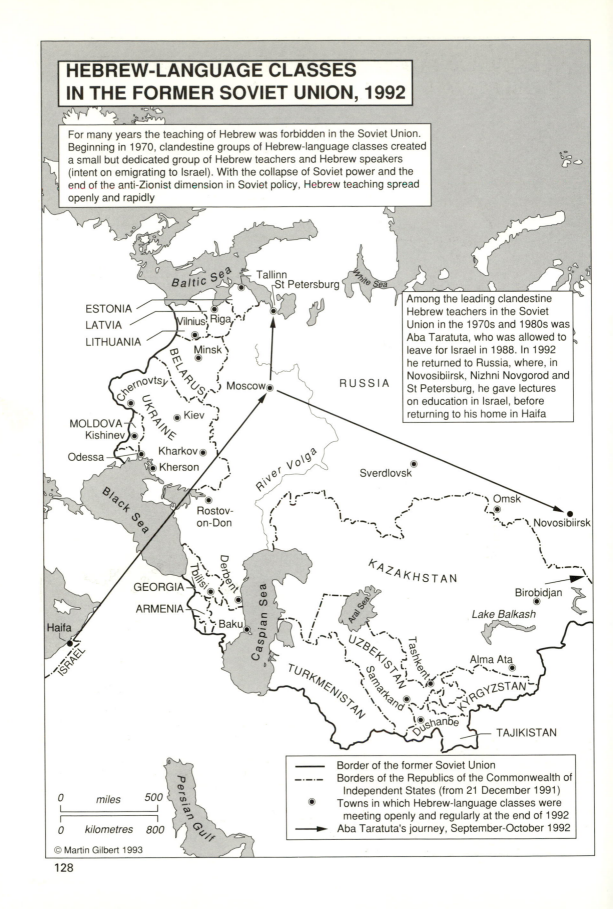

HEBREW-LANGUAGE CLASSES IN THE FORMER SOVIET UNION, 1992

For many years the teaching of Hebrew was forbidden in the Soviet Union. Beginning in 1970, clandestine groups of Hebrew-language classes created a small but dedicated group of Hebrew teachers and Hebrew speakers (intent on emigrating to Israel). With the collapse of Soviet power and the end of the anti-Zionist dimension in Soviet policy, Hebrew teaching spread openly and rapidly

Among the leading clandestine Hebrew teachers in the Soviet Union in the 1970s and 1980s was Aba Taratuta, who was allowed to leave for Israel in 1988. In 1992 he returned to Russia, where, in Novosibiirsk, Nizhni Novgorod and St Petersburg, he gave lectures on education in Israel, before returning to his home in Haifa

Baltic Sea

Tallinn
St Petersburg
White Sea

ESTONIA
LATVIA
LITHUANIA

Vilnius
Riga

Minsk

BELARUS

RUSSIA

Chernovtsy

Moscow

Kiev

UKRAINE

MOLDOVA
Kishinev

Odessa
Kharkov
Kherson

River Volga

Sverdlovsk

Black Sea

Rostov-on-Don

Omsk

Novosibiirsk

KAZAKHSTAN

Derbent

Tbilisi

GEORGIA

ARMENIA

Baku

Caspian Sea

Birobidjan

Lake Balkash

Haifa

ISRAEL

TURKMENISTAN

Aral Sea

UZBEKISTAN

Tashkent

Alma Ata

Samarkand

KYRGYZSTAN

Dushanbe

TAJIKISTAN

Persian Gulf

| 0 | miles | 500 |
| 0 | kilometres | 800 |

─────── Border of the former Soviet Union

─·─·─·─ Borders of the Republics of the Commonwealth of Independent States (from 21 December 1991)

⊙ Towns in which Hebrew-language classes were meeting openly and regularly at the end of 1992

───► Aba Taratuta's journey, September-October 1992

© Martin Gilbert 1993

HEBREW-LANGUAGE NEWSPAPERS AND LIBRARIES IN THE FORMER SOVIET UNION, 1992

In the 25 years before the Bolshevik revolution of 1917, Hebrew-language newspapers, and libraries of Jewish books, were a feature of Russian-Jewish life. Banned for 70 years, such newspapers and libraries began to re-appear with the collapse of Soviet Communism. Following the disintegration of the Soviet Union (on 21 December 1991) such newspapers and libraries again became a feature of Jewish life for 1,600,000 Jews throughout the Commonwealth of Independent States. By the end of 1992, 53 Jewish newspapers were being published

Baltic Sea

Sverdlovsk

Tallinn ❷
ESTONIA

St. Petersburg ❻

Riga ◉▲
LATVIA
LITHUANIA
Vilnius ❷◉
Minsk ❷
◉▲
BELARUS
Bobruisk ◉

Moscow ◉▲
⓫

RUSSIA

Samara ◉

River Volga

Also: ➡
Tashkent
Birobidjan ❹
Samarkand

Lvov ◉▲
Kiev ◉▲ ❷
UKRAINE
Kharkov ◉
Chernovtsy ❺ ◉
Donetsk◉
Dnepropetrovsk ◉
Kishinev ◉▲

Black Sea

Caspian Sea

GEORGIA
Tbilisi ❷ ◉▲
ARMENIA
AZERBAIJAN
Baku ▲ ❷

Aegean Sea

Mediterranean Sea

—	borders of the Soviet Union, 1945-1991
—·—·—	borders of the Republics of the Commonwealth of Independent States (from 21 December 1991)
◉	Towns in which Hebrew-language newspapers were being published on a regular basis by the end of 1992 (with the number of papers, when more than 1, in a black circle)
▲	Towns with Jewish libraries

| 0 | kilometres | 500 |
| 0 | miles | 300 |

© Martin Gilbert 1993

● Jerusalem

Persian Gulf

ANTI-SEMITIC INCIDENTS IN EUROPE, 1992

The year 1992 saw an increase in anti-semitic incidents throughout Europe, where there were also mass demonstrations against neo-Nazi violence, and Government pronouncements against anti-semitism. In the newly-united Germany, where 368,000 foreigners had found asylum by the end of 1992, the main violence was against Turkish, Kurdish, Arab, Armenian, Spanish, and Vietnamese immigrants, also against Gypsies

2 November
52 Jewish gravestones overturned

21 October
Concentration camp memorial overturned

27 September
Concentration camp memorial partly destroyed

30 August
Holocaust memorial vandalised

21 December
Jewish cemetery desecrated

20 July
A pig's head taken to the synagogue with the slogan "death to the Jews"

4 November
90 out of 190 graves vandalised in the Jewish cemetery

9 December
a Neo-Nazi imprisoned for 32 months as a "grave danger" to immigrants and Jews

14 November
150,000 protest against anti-semitic and anti-foreigner violence

8 May
A publisher who said that gas chambers did not exist imprisoned for 18 months

20 September
While in Jerusalem, the Hungarian President calls for international solidarity against the resurgence of racism

4 November
Magazine attack on Jews for having too much influence

1 December
synagogue desecrated

4 November
Jewish graves vandalised

1 November
Jewish gravestones vandalised

3 November
Neo-Nazis deface Jewish shops with Star of David signs

6 November
30,000 Italians march in protest against anti-Semitism

1 March
hand grenade thrown at synagogue: a blind beggar injured

SWEDEN
Stockholm

Baltic Sea

GERMANY
Ravensbrück
Sachsenhausen
Wuppertal
Bonn
Erfurt
Rudolstadt
Cottbus
Leipzig

FRANCE
Strasbourg

Vienna
Eisenstadt
AUSTRIA
Budapest
HUNGARY

Ferrara
ITALY
Rome
Adriatic Sea

Black Sea

TURKEY
Istanbul

0   kilometres   250

0   miles   150

© Martin Gilbert 1993

ANTI-SEMITIC INCIDENTS IN THE FORMER SOVIET UNION, 1992

Despite Boris Yeltsin's decree against anti-semitism of October 1991, anti-Jewish feelings rose to the surface in many Republics of the former Soviet Union in 1992. This served as a spur to emigration to Israel, the United States and even Germany. Throughout the Commonwealth of Independent States, however, Jewish cultural life flourished, as it had not done since the Bolshevik revolution in 1917

6 July
An anti-semitic article published in the newspaper *Yurmala*

12 February
The poet Evgeni Yevtushenko warns against anti-semitism "a genetic disease: in some situations an incubus could be resurrected"

17 February
Members of the Orthodox Lubavich movement beaten up

5 April
Lubavich headquarters fire-bombed

13 August
Anti-semitic taunts against Jewish school children

July
Jews assaulted in the streets

7 August
Report reaches the West of the murder of a Jew, identified only as 'Moshe'

May
Two Jews, Eduard Azizov and Gandi Goldov tortured and killed

May
Jewish cemeteries vandalised; public demonstrations against Jews

July-August
Attacks on synagogues and on individual Jews

August
Physical attacks, and newspaper articles against Jews all month

1 September
A Jew murdered by anti-semites

Barents Sea
Baltic Sea
White Sea
Riga
LATVIA
Lvov
Kiev
UKRAINE
Kharkov
Moscow
RUSSIA
Perm
Black Sea
Mahachkala
Derbent
Baku
Caspian Sea
Aral Sea
AZERBAIJAN
Mediterranean
Jerusalem
TAJIKISTAN
Dushanbe

0   miles   300
0   kilometres   500

—— Borders of the Soviet Union, 1945-1991

—·— Borders of the Republics of the Commonwealth of Independent States (founded 21 December 1991)

© Martin Gilbert, 1993

131

THE JEWS OF THE FORMER YUGOSLAVIA, 1992

On the eve of the Second World War there were 72,000 Jews in Yugoslavia. Of these, 60,000 were murdered, some by the German occupation forces, others by Croat Ustachi forces. Jews were active in the Communist resistance and in post-war reconstruction. At the time of the break-up of Yugoslavia, with the Slovene and Croat declarations of independence on 25 June 1991, most Jews were living in Belgrade, Zagreb and Sarajevo. More than a hundred small village communities had been destroyed in the Second World War

AUSTRIA

HUNGARY

RUMANIA

SLOVENIA

Ljubljana
20

Zagreb
1,500

CROATIA

River Danube

Novi Sad
200

Belgrade
2,000

BOSNIA

Zenica
30

Sarajevo
700

Mostar
30

SERBIA

Split
200

Adriatic Sea

to Britain
100

Dalmatian Coast

to Spain
200

to Israel
500

BULGARIA

Skopje
100

MACEDONIA

ITALY

In 1992 more than 800 Jews fled from the fighting in the former Yugoslav Republics. Almost all of them expressed their desire to return to their homes when the fighting ended

ALBANIA

On 10 February 1993 the Israeli Government agreed to take in 84 Muslims seeking a safe haven from the fighting in Bosnia

GREECE

———	Yugoslav border, 1945-1991
—·—·—	Borders of the Republics, 1992
←—	Jewish refugees from the fighting, 1992

0   kilometres   160

0   miles   100

© Martin Gilbert 1993

Bibliography

The following bibliography is strictly selective. It consists of some eighty books which I myself have found useful while gathering material for the maps.

In addition to the books listed below, I have made frequent use of a number of general reference works, of which the most valuable were:

Isodore Singer (Managing Editor), *The Jewish Encyclopaedia*, 12 vols., New York, 1901–1906, the most comprehensive of all encyclopaedias on Jewish affairs.

Y. L. Katzenelson (Editor), *Yevreyskaya Entsiklopediya*, 16 vols., St. Petersburg, 1906–1913. An essential source for all problems of Russian Jewry.

Encyclopaedia Judaica, 16 vols. (Jerusalem, 1972). The most recent complete multi-volume encyclopaedia of Jewish history.

Cecil Roth (Editor-in-Chief), *The Standard Jewish Encyclopaedia*, one volume (New York, 1962). The fullest single-volume work of reference.

Israeli Department of Surveys and the Bialik Institute, *Atlas of Israel* (Jerusalem, 1956), contains an excellent bibliography of over a thousand cartographic sources relating to Israel.

General works on Jewish History

Nathan Ausubel, *Pictorial History of the Jewish People* (New York, 1954)

Salo W. Baron, *A Social and Religious History of the Jews* (New York, 1952–1960)

Edwyn R. Bevan and Charles Singer (editors), *The Legacy of Israel* (Oxford, 1927)

Max I. Dimont, *Jews, God and History* (New York, 1962)

Max L. Margolis and A. Marx, *A History of the Jewish People* (Philadelphia, 1964)

James William Parkes, *A History of the Jewish People* (London, 1962)

Cecil Roth, *A Short History of the Jewish People* (London, 1959)

Cecil Roth, *Personalities and Events in Jewish History* (Philadelphia, 1961)

Biblical and Classical Periods

W. F. Albright, *New Horizons in Biblical Research* (London, 1966)

M. Avi-Yonah, *Map of Roman Palestine* (Oxford, 1940)

Daniel-Rops, *Israel and the Ancient World* (Paris, 1943; London, 1949)

Luc Grollenberg, *Atlas de la Bible* (London, 1956)

James Hastings, *Dictionary of the Bible* (London, 1963)

Jean Juster, *Les Juifs dans l'empire romain* (Paris, 1914)

Harry J. Leon, *The Jews of Ancient Rome* (Philadelphia, 1960)

Benjamin Maisler, *Historical Atlas of Palestine* (Jerusalem, 1942)

W. O. E. Osterley, *The Jews and Judaism During the Greek Period* (London, 1941)

John William Parkes, *Jesus, Paul and the Jews* (London, 1936)

George Adam Smith, *Historical Geography of the Holy Land* (London, 1894)

John Stirling, *An Atlas of the Life of Christ* (London, 1954)

John Stirling, *An Atlas Illustrating the Acts of the Apostles and the Epistles* (London, 1954)

Yigael Yadin, *Masada* (London, 1965)

Yigael Yadin, *Bar-Kokhba* (London, 1971)

Medieval Period

Marcus Nathan Adler, *The Itinery of Benjamin of Tudela* (London, 1907)

George K. Anderson, *The Legend of the Wandering Jew* (Providence, 1965)

Salo Baron, *The Jewish Community; Its History and Structure* (Philadelphia, 1942)

Herbert Ivan Bloom, *The Economic Activities of the Jews of Amsterdam* (Williamsport, 1937)

Claude Reignier Conder, *The Latin Kingdom of Jerusalem 1099–1291* (London, 1897)

D. M. Dunlop, *The History of the Jewish Khazars* (Princeton, 1954)

Louis Finkelstein, *Jewish Self-Government in the Middle Ages* (New York, 1924)

Walter Joseph Fischel, *Jews in the Economic and Political Life of Medieval Islam* (London, 1937)

Solomon Grayzel, *The Church and the Jews in the Thirteenth Century* (New York, 1966)

Julius H. Greenstone, *The Messianic Idea in Jewish History* (Philadelphia, 1906)

Henry Kamen, *The Spanish Inquisition* (London, 1965)

Robert S. Lopez and Irving W. Raymond (eds.), *Medieval Trade in the Mediterranean World* (New York, 1955)

Leon Nemoy, *Karaite Anthology* (New Haven, 1952)

Abraham A. Neuman, *The Jews in Spain* (Philadelphia, 1944)

James William Parkes, *The Conflict of the Church and the Synagogue* (London, 1934)

David Philipson, *Old European Jewries* (Harrisburg, 1894)

L. Rabinowitz, *Jewish Merchant Adventurers* (London, 1948)

Cecil Roth, *The History of the Jews of Italy* (Philadelphia, 1946)

Cecil Roth, *A History of the Marranos* (Philadelphia, 1942)

Cecil Roth, *A History of the Jews in England* (Oxford, 1941)

Cecil Roth, *The Jews of Medieval Oxford* (Oxford, 1951)

Steven Runciman, *A History of the Crusades* (Cambridge, 1951)

Abba Hillel Silver, *A History of Messianic Speculation in Israel* (New York, 1927)

Joshua Starr, *Jews in the Byzantine Empire 641–1204* (Athens, 1939)

Joshua Starr, *Romania, the Jews of the Levant After the Fourth Crusade* (Paris, 1949)

William Charles White, *Chinese Jews* (Toronto, 1942)

Louis Wirth, *The Ghetto* (Chicago, 1928)

Modern Period

Reuben Ainsztein, *Jewish Resistance in Nazi-Occupied Eastern Europe* (London, 1974)

Karl Baedeker, *Austria-Hungary* (Leipzig, 1905)

Salo Baron, *The Russian Jew Under Tsars and Soviets* (New York, 1964)

Norman Bentwich, *They Found Refuge* (London, 1956)

Randolph S. Churchill and Winston S. Churchill, *The Six Day War* (London, 1967)

Israel Cohen, *A Short History of Zionism* (London, 1951)

Israel Cohen, *Contemporary Jewry* (London, 1950)

Israel Cohen, *Vilna* (Philadelphia, 1943)

Israel Cohen, *My Mission to Poland 1918–1919* (London, 1951)

Norman Cohn, *Warrant for Genocide* (London, 1967)

Moshe Dayan, *Diary of the Sinai Campaign* (London, 1966)

S. M. Dubnow, *History of the Jews in Russia and Poland* (Philadelphia, 1916–20)

Abba Eban, *Voice of Israel* (London, 1958)

Lloyd P. Gartner, *The Jewish Immigrant in England 1870–1914* (London, 1960)

Martin Gilbert, *The Jews of Arab Lands: Their History in Maps* (London, 1975)

Martin Gilbert, *The Jews of Russia and the Soviet Union: Their History in Maps* (London, 1976)

Louis Greenberg, *The Jews in Russia: The Struggle for Emancipation* (New Haven 1944 and 1951)

Philip Guedalla, *Napoleon and Palestine* (London, 1925)

Vladimir Jabotinsky, *The Story of the Jewish Legion* (New York, 1954)

Leo Jung (ed.), *Jewish Leaders 1750–1940* (Jerusalem, 1964)

Roderick Kedward, *The Dreyfus Affair* (London, 1964)

Mordechai E. Kreinin, *Israel and Africa* (New York, 1964)

Harry S. Linfield, *Statistics of Jews 1931* (New York, 1931)

Vivian David Lipman, *Social History of the Jews in England 1850–1950* (London, 1954)

Macmillan (publishers), *Atlas of the Arab World and the Middle East* (London, 1960)

Raphael Mahler, *A History of Modern Jewry 1780–1815* (London, 1971)

Arthur D. Morse, *While Six Million Died* (London, 1968)

Alfred Nossig, *Materialen Zur statistik der Judischen Stammes* (Vienna, 1897)

Edgar O'Ballance, *The Arab-Israeli War 1948* (London, 1956)

F. J. Pietri, *Napoléon et les Israélites* (Paris, 1965)

James William Parkes, *Arabs and Jews in the Middle East: a Tragedy of Errors* (London, 1967)

J. H. Patterson, *With the Judaeans in the Palestine Campaign* (London, 1922)

Leon Poliakov, *Harvest of Hate* (New York, 1954)

Malcolm J. Proudfoot, *European Refugees 1939–52* (London, 1957)

Peter George J. Pulzer, *The Rise of Political Anti-Semitism in Germany and Austria* (New York, 1964)

Gerald Reitlinger, *The Final Solution* (London, 1953)

Emmanuel Ringelblum, *Polish-Jewish Relations during the Second World War* (Jerusalem, 1974)

Adolf Rudnicki, *Ascent to Heaven* (London, 1951)

Harry Sacher, *Zionist Portraits* (London, 1959)

Joseph B. Schechtman, *On Wings of Eagles* (New York, 1961)

A. J. Sherman, *Island Refuge* (London, 1974)

Yuri Suhl (ed.), *They Fought Back* (London, 1968)

Christopher Sykes, *Cross Roads to Israel* (London, 1965)

M. U. Schappes, *A Documentary History of the Jews in the United States 1654–1875* (New York, 1950)

Leonard Stein, *The Balfour Declaration* (London, 1966)

Arieh Tartakower and Kurt R. Grossman, *The Jewish Refugee* (New York, 1944)

Chaim Weizmann, *Trial and Error* (London, 1952)

Israel Zangwill, *Children of the Ghetto* (London, 1892)